WOW!
Resumes
Administrative Careers

WOW!
Resumes
Administrative Careers

How to Put Together a Winning Resume

Rachel Lefkowitz

McGraw-Hill

New York San Francisco Washington, D.C. Auckland Bogotá
Caracas Lisbon London Madrid Mexico City Milan
Montreal New Delhi San Juan Singapore
Sydney Tokyo Toronto

Library of Congress Cataloging-in-Publication Data

Lefkowitz, Rachel.
    WOW! resumes for administrative careers : how to put together a
winning resume / Rachel Lefkowitz.
        p.   cm.
    Includes index.
    ISBN 0-07-037102-4
    1. Résumés (Employment)   I. Title.
  HF5383.L44   1997
808'.06665—dc21   96-38146
                                                                              CIP

McGraw-Hill

A Division of The McGraw-Hill Companies

Copyright © 1997 by Rachel Lefkowitz. All rights reserved. Printed
in the United States of America. Except as permitted under the
United States Copyright Act of 1976, no part of this publication may
be reproduced or distributed in any form or by any means, or stored
in a database or retrieval system, without the prior written
permission of the publisher.

5 6 7 8 9 0 MAL/MAL 0 9 8 7 6 5 4 3

ISBN 0-07-0387102-4 (pbk.)

*The sponsoring editor for this book was Betsy Brown, the assistant editor
was Danielle Bauer, the editing supervisor was Fred Dahl, and the
production supervisor was Suzanne W. B. Rapcavage. It was set in Stone
Serif by Inkwell Publishing Services.*

Printed and bound by Malloy Lithography.

McGraw-Hill books are available at special quantity discounts to use
as premiums and sales promotions, or for use in corporate training
sessions. For more information, please write to the Director of Special
Sales, McGraw-Hill, 11 West 19th Street, New York, NY 10011. Or
contact your local bookstore.

Contents

Preface   *ix*

Acknowledgments   *x*

Introduction—how to make your resume stand out from all the rest   *1*

1 Basic resume format—fundamentals you need to get started   *4*

The makings of a resume   *4*

Five seconds to get noticed—make it a great first impression   *5*

Clear, clean, and crisp   *6*

Margins, spacing, and structure   *7*

One page is better than two   *8*

The chronological resume—what employers like best   *9*

In conclusion   *9*

2 The introductory sections—hook an employer in the first few lines of your resume   *10*

Your name, address, and phone number   *10*

The Job Objective—knowing what you want and showing it   *11*

The Summary of Qualifications—creating an immediate impact   *16*

Tailor it for a perfect job fit—how to match your skills to an employer's exact needs   *20*

Summary of Qualifications do's and don'ts   *25*

Beyond the want ads—utilizing all your job resources   *26*

In conclusion   *26*

3 Job History—give yours an incredible professional polish   *27*

Dates of employment and position titles—handling the nitty gritties   *28*

The Main Function—revealing the full scope of your job   *30*

Your job duties—turn weak old duties into powerful job descriptions   *32*

The phrase-building formula   *34*

Spice up the simplest clerical tasks   *40*

Adding the human touch   *41*

Special achievements—how to find and flaunt them   *42*

Enhance it all with positive employer comments   *45*

From plain words to powerful verbs—your key word list   *45*

Organizing your job duties   *48*

Organizing your job positions—keep tailoring your Job History to the job you're applying for now   *50*

In conclusion   *51*

4 Education and training—how to present yours best   *52*

Educational credentials can help support you for the job you want   *52*

What to put in   *53*

What to leave out   *54*

Education or Job History—which comes first?   *55*

Forming your educational listing   *57*

In conclusion   *58*

5 Technical skills and special abilities—dazzle an employer with a showcase of your skills   *59*

Stop taking your skills for granted   *59*

Discovering your dynamic skills   *62*

You have more technical skills than you think—how to find and use them all   *62*

Your fabulous special abilities—learn how to identify them   *66*

Finding your characteristic features   *69*

Putting it all together—beat the competition in one fell swoop   *72*

Stay on top—keeping up with the hottest skills of today and tomorrow   *74*

In conclusion   *75*

6 The end sections—hang in there, you're almost done   *76*

Languages—optional but valuable   *76*

Memberships—that little extra that can mean a lot   *78*

Leave out the outdated for a stronger, more focused resume   *80*

References—what they are and how to use them   *82*

Excellent reference letters—if you've got them, flaunt them!   *86*

In conclusion   *86*

7 New grads, career changers, and all types of special situations—how to conquer your resume problems and beat the competition *87*

Dispel your worries   *88*

The Functional Style Resume—why it can overcome almost anything   *88*

Career changers—from "unlikely candidate" to "good match for the job"   *92*

New grads—from "inexperienced novice" to "good solid candidate"   *97*

Individuals reentering the workforce—how to avoid looking outdated   *101*

Overqualifieds—how to look just right for the job you want *now*   *103*

Irrelevant job positions—when you have too many or they're in the wrong place   *104*

Employment gaps—how to stop them from sticking out   *106*

Short-term job positions—how to avoid looking like a job hopper   *107*

In conclusion   *109*

8 From mediocre to magnificent—sixteen sample resumes transformed *110*

Presenting … the before and afters   *111*

   1. Secretary/Receptionist   *112*

   2. Medical Secretary   *115*

   3. Legal Secretary   *118*

   4. Legal Secretary   *121*

   5. Executive Secretary/Administrative Assistant   *126*

   6. Administrative Assistant   *129*

   7. Accounts Receivable Clerk   *132*
      Secretary/Office Clerk   *135*

   8. Customer Service Clerk   *136*
      Accounting Clerk   *140*

   9. Customer Service Representative   *142*

 10. Data Entry Operator   *146*

 11. Data Processor   *149*

 12. Bookkeeper   *152*

 13. Medical Secretary—New Grad   *155*

 14. Receptionist—Career Changer   *158*

 15. Financial Clerk—Reentering the Workforce   *161*

 16. Office Clerk (Overqualified)   *163*
      Office Manager   *166*

What a difference   *167*

Tailoring your whole resume—the key to resume success   *167*

More to the sample resumes than meets the eye—still more tips and advice to gain   *167*

Prove what you say you are—how to back up your Summary of Qualifications throughout your resume   *167*

How to make yourself look great even when you're not perfect   *170*

How to modify your tailored resume to fit any job position   *171*

In conclusion   *172*

9 Preparing the final draft   *173*

Checklist—did you do it right?   *173*

Last-minute extras   *176*

Tips for saving resume space   *176*

Polishing and tightening   *178*

Don't fall into the spelling trap   *178*

Proofreading—review it once, twice, and over again   *179*

In conclusion   *179*

10 The cover letter—preparing your dynamite resume companion   *180*

Problem cover letters and how to avoid them   *181*

The ideal cover letter—clear and simple plus attention-getting appeal   *182*

Basic cover letter format—fundamentals you need to get started   *182*

The cover letter parts   *184*

Making it error free   *187*

The sample phrases—your invaluable cover letter writing tool   *188*

Five sample cover letters—how all the parts come together   *191*

Cover letter do's and don'ts   *197*

Checklist—did you do it right?   *197*

In conclusion   *198*

11 Simply divine and ready to go—what to do with your resume package   *199*

Faxing your resume   *199*

Mailing your resume   *200*

Making sure it arrived   *201*

Making the call—professional and businesslike always   *201*

Preparing to receive an employer's call   *201*

In conclusion   *201*

Conclusion—updating your resume—now and in the future   *202*

Appendix—your guide to professional associations   *203*

Index   *206*

Preface

If you want a resume that will get you noticed, get you interviews, and help you get that office job—you have picked up the perfect book!

Despite today's fierce job competition, you can sell all of your skills, qualities, talents, and achievements—successfully, to an employer—in one exciting resume page. The instructions in this book will show you how, and guide you effortlessly through the process.

In this challenging job market, resume guides line bookstore shelves by the dozen. There are general resume books and specialized ones for all kinds of occupations including teachers, scientists, engineers, technicians, health professionals, sales personnel, executives, and attorneys. But there is no resume guide geared to secretaries or clerical workers, one of the largest occupations of the U.S. economy, consisting of 20 million office jobs.

WOW! Resumes for Administrative Careers, however, is specially designed for you. If you are an office worker of any kind—an executive, legal, or medical secretary, an administrative assistant, office manager, receptionist, word processing or data entry operator, customer service representative, bookkeeper, financial or general office clerk—whether you already have a resume or you're just starting one from scratch, this book will arm you with everything you need to create a targeted, top-notch resume that stands above all the rest.

Consisting of more than just the general advice and instruction of other resume books, *WOW! Resumes for Administrative Careers* is loaded with precise details, samples, and examples all specially geared to the office worker. It shows you how to present yourself powerfully and professionally by giving yourself full credit for everything you know and do. It provides you with innovative leading-edge strategies and teaches you how to replace "one-size-fits-all" resumes that no longer work with resumes that are precisely tailored to employers' specific needs—a new resume approach that is crucial for winning attention in today's tough job market.

Even if you're a new grad, if you've become a career changer, or if you face any other type of special situation, you too can gain great tips and techniques to put your resume on top.

And—I promise—this book will make it easy for you. I will take you by the hand and guide you through each and every step of your resume preparation.

You've already picked up this book to take that first, most important step. Read on, and in no time, you'll be on your way to producing your fabulous WOW resume!

Acknowledgments

I wish to express my appreciation to several people. I would like to thank Betsy Brown, McGraw-Hill Senior Editor, and Danielle Bauer, Assistant Editor. Also, many thanks to my resume clients who allowed their resumes to be used in this book. Special thanks go to my family for all their support, and especially to Jack, Sarale, and Dani—for your love and patience, and putting up with my hectic writing schedule.

Rachel Lefkowitz

Introduction

How to Make Your Resume Stand Out from All the Rest

You're a secretary. You type, file, and answer phones. You need a job, so you whip up a resume that says you're a secretary and that you know how to type, file, and answer phones. You include a bunch of previous jobs you've held and send the resume off to a prospective employer. You figure this resume will help you land a job interview. After all, it gives an employer a decent, accurate presentation of yourself. Right?

Wrong.

You are not just a secretary. You are the office lifeline. You're an administrative assistant, public relations manager, telecommunications supervisor, bookkeeper, word processing specialist, and computer operator. The daily business of an office pumps through you like blood through a heart.

Typing, filing, and answering phones are simplified, lifeless descriptions of the duties you really perform. If you carefully analyzed every aspect of your clerical experience, you'd be surprised at how much you really do and what your abilities include.

Today's secretary/office worker is at the forefront of an office automation revolution and is capable of a multitude of technical skills and abilities like never before. Even traditional duties have taken on a new image. It's time to stop oversimplifying your job duties and underestimating your skills. It's time to excise those dry, generalized phrases from your resume and the weak images that go along with them.

Instead, learn to shine, dazzle, and amaze. Shine with polished descriptions of your greatest assets and achievements. Dazzle employers with your unique skills and abilities. Amaze them and yourself with the extent of your professional and technical knowledge. Best of all, learn to beat today's fierce competition with a top-notch resume that zeros in on an employer's exact needs.

Whether you're a secretary or clerical worker with twenty years of experience or a new graduate, you can exceed hundreds of other job seekers with this book.

You will learn how to:

- Create an attractive, attention-getting resume.
- Hook an employer's interest in the first few lines of your resume by utilizing the most up-to-date resume formats and techniques.
- Enhance all job descriptions with powerful, professional wording using a step-by-step phrase-building formula and word lists.
- Transform even menial job tasks into impressive information.
- Discover skills, talents, and achievements you never even knew you had and learn how to show them off.
- Custom tailor your resume to specific job positions using a unique tailoring approach employers find hard to resist.
- Camouflage problems or shortcomings with special resume styles and tips.
- Create a dynamite, attention-getting cover letter.

In addition, this book is packed with invaluable samples and special features including:

- Visual resume guides that build your resume right along with you.
- Sixteen real-life before and after winning sample resumes for all types of clerical jobs.
- Instructions for chronological and functional style formats to help you organize a resume that is best for your situation and lets you sell yourself most effectively.
- Innovative strategies for new grads, career changers, individuals reentering the workforce, overqualified individuals, and others.
- Ready-made cover letter phrases to mix and match for an instant cover letter.
- Checklists to help you make sure your resume's on track, and much more.

Proven winning strategies together with easy-to-follow instructions and straightforward examples make this your ultimate resume writing guide. Now, get ready: Together, we're going to create your best resume ever.

1

Basic Resume Format

Fundamentals You Need to Get Started

Let's start from the beginning. Before you can enhance your image, boast your achievements, or sell your assets, you must first understand the very basics—what a resume is and how a resume looks.

In this chapter, you will learn about the basic parts or ingredients that make up a resume and how you can structure those parts in a clear, attractive format to make a great first impression.

The Makings of a Resume

Resume writing is not as difficult or daunting a task as it may initially seem. In fact, once you understand what resumes are all about, it really becomes quite simple.

Pretend resumes didn't exist. Suppose you could just call up employers personally to persuade them to hire you. What would you say?

You would likely describe your last job or some previous positions you've held because many duties you performed there are important to the job you want. You might discuss your training, tell the employer a bit about who you are, including your good qualities and skills you have for the job, and you might offer phone numbers of previous employers who you know will say good things about you to back you up.

All these things are the makings of a resume. A resume is not a meaningless document solely invented to make job hunters' lives a tedious chore. On the contrary, a resume makes the job of selling yourself easy. It takes all the information you need to give to an employer—your professional and academic achievements—and organizes it into clear, readable parts. These resume parts are as follows:

1. *Job Objective*—Simply and clearly tells an employer the position you are applying for.

2. *Summary of Qualifications*—Gives an employer a quick rundown of the desirable skills and features you possess.

3. *Employment History*—Tells an employer all the previous relevant positions you've held and the duties you performed.

4. *Education*—Covers your educational background and relevant training.

5. *Technical Skills and Special Abilities*—Details your technical skills and specialized knowledge.

6. *References*—Indicates that references are available.

That's it. That's your whole resume. Nothing too difficult or scary. We will delve into the contents of these resume parts later, but first, on to your resume's initial drawing factor—its physical appearance.

Five Seconds to Get Noticed—Make It a Great First Impression

Let's concentrate on the first element of your resume that can make or break your chance of success: its layout and appearance. An employer may never bother reading your resume if it doesn't look worth his or her time.

Imagine an employer's desk, hundreds of resumes strewn about. A big job awaits her; she has to plow through it all. Meanwhile, she has a vacant position, an inexperienced temp, and an office in utter chaos. She needs to find someone fast. Similarly, imagine a hiring manager whose job is to review hundreds of resumes and recruit job applicants day in and day out. By now, he's turned five-second resume scanning into an art form.

Naturally, the first resumes these employers will eliminate are the uninviting kind such as sloppy resumes, marginless resumes, and resumes that are downright difficult to read due to small print, light print, cluttered print, or unorganized text.

Resume layout and appearance are critical. A clear, attractive resume has the power to draw immediate attention and create a respectable impression of the resume writer. It shows you took the time to make it perfect—which earns points in your favor right from the start.

Clear, Clean, and Crisp

Yours can be the crisp white resume with sharp bold print screaming "read me" from under the mass of resumes on an employer's desk. Remember, your resume provides an employer with a first impression of you. Demand attention with striking good looks. You dress to impress on a job interview; so, too, you should groom your resume.

See Fig. 1-1. Notice the placement of information and overall appearance of the Basic Resume Format sample.

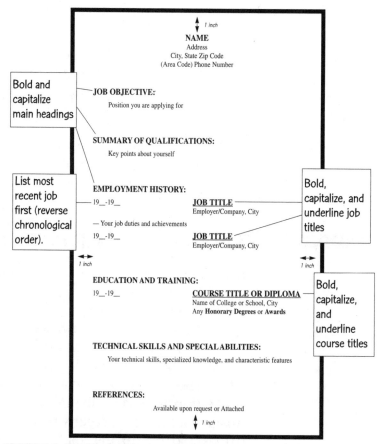

FIGURE 1-1. **Basic Resume Format.**

This resume uses the three c's—clear, clean, and crisp—to create the most attractive readable format.

Clear

Grab the eye with big, bold headings. They break up the monotonous look of one continuous typeface to form clear, distinguishable sections.

All main headings such as Job Objective, Summary of Qualifications, etc., are capitalized and typed in bold. As well, subheadings such as job titles and course titles are also capitalized, typed in bold, and underlined because these main facts about yourself should stand out. For instance, "**<u>SECRETARY TO DIRECTOR</u>**" draws more attention than "Secretary to Director." Essential information gets noticed at a glance.

Clean

Make sure you have clean space or proportionate empty space. Don't overcrowd your resume with too much material. Just as you can't feel comfortable in cluttered surroundings, you can't comfortably read a cluttered resume.

Crisp

Use high-quality white bond paper with sharp black print.

A laser printer will give you the best print quality. Its output is dark and crisp, and it is an excellent choice for your resume. The inkjet is next in the lineup of quality printers. It can give you comparable results to the laser but upon close inspection, you may detect a difference. Last is the dot-matrix. It works much the way a typewriter does, but cannot produce text as sharp as the laser or the inkjet.

FIGURE 1-2.

White paper is the most appropriate choice for your resume. It has a professional business look that allows the text to stand out best; however, neutral colors such as off-white, light beige, light gray, or buff are also acceptable.

Make sure to use standard 8½ × 11 inch sheets of paper that are at least 20-pound bond for a substantial look and feel.

Margins, Spacing, and Structure

These are the general guidelines to follow:

- Leave a one-inch (2.5 cm) margin all around the page (left, right, top, and bottom).
- Double- or triple-space between major resume sections. Double-space after headings or between paragraphs of information within sections.

Feel free to make necessary adjustments such as altering spacing or indentations depending on the type of print and the amount of text you have.

If you wish to use varying styles, go ahead. For instance, instead of placing all your headings at the left-hand margin, you may want to center your headings as in Fig. 1-3.

Due to new graphic options and the advanced capabilities of computers and printers, interesting fonts and large amounts of text can be positioned on paper attractively and professionally. If you have access to a computer and printer that will give you this type of versatility, go ahead and experiment but *don't*:

NAME
Address
City
Phone Number

JOB OBJECTIVE

SUMMARY OF QUALIFICATIONS

EMPLOYMENT HISTORY

FIGURE 1-3.

- Use extra-fancy typestyles like script or italics to make up the typeface of your whole resume. These are not as readable or businesslike as standard typefaces.

- Use outrageously large print as an attention-getting gimmick. An entire resume set in huge print is not pleasing to the eye, may actually distract the reader from the content, and unnecessarily takes up valuable resume space. (Note, however, that italics or larger print can be attractive and effective when used for resume headings.)

- Stray far from the required basic setup of a resume. When choosing resume fonts and layout, it's generally better to stick with a safer, more traditional approach than risk putting off any potential employers.

One Page Is Better Than Two

When it comes to resume length, the shorter the better. The key is to sell yourself to the maximum while keeping your resume as trimmed and to-the-point as possible. This doesn't mean, however, that you should cram everything together or eliminate important information because you have reached the one-page boundary.

A one-page resume is ideal, but if you must, you can go further. If you feel that vital information will not adequately fit onto one page, go on to a second, but try to make one and three quarter pages your absolute limit.

The Chronological Resume—What Employers Like Best

Our basic resume format sample is in reverse chronological order—a straightforward style that employers appreciate most. It is organized in order of occurrence, last thing first or your most recent job first.

If you are a clerical worker with a solid relevant work history, the chronological resume will complement you just fine. If, however, you are a new grad or career changer with little or no clerical experience, or face any other types of resume problems such as employment gaps, short-term jobs, irrelevant jobs, being overqualified, or reentering the workforce after a lengthy absence, pay special attention to Chapter 7, "New Grads, Career Changers, and All Types of Special Situations—How to Conquer Your Resume Problems and Beat the Competition," for style variations, such as the functional style resume, and special tips to present yourself most favorably.

In Conclusion

Now that you know how the basic resume looks and what its parts are made up of, it's time to dig into the actual resume and begin its construction. Tailoring techniques, phrase-building formulas, word lists, and precise clerical samples and examples all await.

Starting from the very top of the resume page with your name, address, and phone number, Chapter 2, "The Introductory Sections" is next.

2

The Introductory Sections

Hook an Employer in the First Few Lines of Your Resume

Okay. Time to create your resume parts. First, visualize that employer and hiring manager again. What was it they were doing? Oh yes, scanning those resumes, hundreds of them in fact, one after another. Face it: An employer's time is extremely limited. You have to do all you can to get your resume noticed right away, or it might not get noticed at all. This chapter will show you how to start your resume off right.

You'll learn to gain immediate attention by appealing directly to an employer's needs. A clear Job Objective and irresistible Summary of Qualifications can do that for you. So take out a clean sheet of paper or flip to a blank computer screen and begin.

Your Name, Address, and Phone Number

Start the rough draft of your resume. First things first, and in this case it's your name, address, and phone number centered at the top of the page.

> **NAME**
> **Address**
> **City, State Zip Code**
> **Phone Number**

FIGURE 2-1.

This is more of a basic reminder than anything else. You'd be surprised that there are actually job hunters out there who ask if they need to include their phone numbers on their resumes. The answer is *Yes.* Definitely. No matter what! How else would an employer be able to contact you quickly and easily?

Here's how it should look:

MARY SMITH
123 Ocean Drive
Miami Beach, FL 10002
(123) 555-1249

Don't forget to center it. Don't forget your area code.

You can get fancy if you like and instead of centering it, do something as shown in Fig. 2-2 or Fig 2-3. Now drop two to three lines and continue.

MARY SMITH
123 Ocean Drive
Miami Beach, FL 10002
(123) 555-1249

FIGURE 2-2.

MARY SMITH
123 Ocean Drive, Miami Beach, FL 10002 (123) 555-1249

FIGURE 2-3.

The Job Objective—Knowing What You Want and Showing It

The Job Objective forms the first line of your resume after your name, address, and phone number. Its purpose is simple but vital. It tells an employer what job you are applying for.

```
                         NAME
                        Address
                   City, State Zip Code
                     Phone Number

JOB OBJECTIVE
```

FIGURE 2-4.

There are many misconceptions about job objectives. "Do I need one at all?... Should I use a general one to keep me open to everything?... Is a job objective the same thing as a career goal?... What *is* a job objective anyway?" These are some of the confusing questions job hunters hound themselves with.

Sit back, relax, and before writing anything, you will learn what a job objective should really do for you and how to avoid inadequate or problem ones. Before long, you'll know how to make your job objective strong and effective and the best for your resume.

Change your mindset—scrap those all-purpose resumes with no job objectives

Probably the most common type of resume is the all-purpose kind. It is produced by you, with the help of a book, a friend, or a professional resume-writing service. It is created with the purpose of sending it out to many different job positions. Thus, it has no job objective, that is, it doesn't state a particular position you're applying for, because it tries to appeal to every type of clerical position out there. Multiple photocopies likely sit in a desk drawer in your home ready to go as soon as another position becomes available. This single, all-purpose resume usually gets accompanied by a cover letter, which is the only thing you ever change. Every time you apply for a new position, you get out the typewriter or flick on the computer and insert into the letter the new position you want. You enclose the cover letter along with one of your photocopied resume clones in an envelope, and voilà, that's your method for creating and sending off resumes into the job world. Pretty neat, huh?

No, it isn't.

Change your mindset! Scrap this type of resume forever!

This resume will get you nowhere in today's job market. One used to be able to get away with this. That's not the case anymore.

First of all, cover letters easily get separated from their resume counterparts. They are not nearly as important as your resume and sometimes don't even get read at all. Why, then, place the only specific information about the job you want in the cover letter and not the resume? Why should the only direct contact between you and the prospective employer go in the cover letter alone? Furthermore, why settle for a resume that is nothing more than a generic document? You can bet an employer won't settle for it.

Second, remind yourself of what you are facing: fewer employment opportunities and the fiercest job competition ever. For every job you apply for, you are literally competing against hundreds of other job applicants.

Your resume needs everything you can possibly give it. You need to give the employer a reason to choose yours over the others. Wake it up. Give it life. Get it noticed. Make your resume speak directly to the employer by giving it a direct, specific job objective. Here's a good example:

JOB OBJECTIVE: To work as an executive secretary

This is a specific job objective because it states the specific position you're applying for. It speaks directly to the employer by responding to the exact position he or she needs filled. It is clear and focused and gives your resume a sense of direction right from the start.

Forget general job objectives that appeal to anything and everything

A resume with a general job objective is not much better than a resume with no job objective at all.

This is another common shortcut job hunters like to take—using a general job objective that tries to encompass every type of position available. For instance, you write, "To work as a secretary" or "To obtain a clerical position" as your job objective and plan to send this out for any and all positions including medical secretary, legal secretary, word processor, administrative assistant, file clerk, accounting clerk, machine transcriptionist—you name it. You'll try them all, and you figure this *one* job objective is good enough to fit them all.

It's not. This approach may save you time, but it will hardly impress an employer. You'll give the appearance that you either don't understand the position, can't be bothered to write an accurate objective, or don't care what you get as long as someone considers you for anything. The resume that tries so hard to appeal to every type of clerical position usually ends up not appealing to any at all.

Specific job objectives give you the edge

Resumes with general job objectives, or worse, no job objectives at all, are the equivalent of sending duplicate letters to friends, each with the same wording with the personal touch missing, specific content missing, and worst of all, the feeling that the letter is not speaking to anyone in particular. Just as a letter to a friend needs individual attention, so does your resume to an employer.

Employers are human too, and they love resumes that speak specifically to them. When you show that you know exactly what you want, through a specific job objective that matches exactly what the employer is looking for—that's impressive.

Invest the time and effort to alter your resume for every different position with a clear, specific job objective and supporting content. This tailored approach will certainly pay off. You will look like a perfect match for every job you apply for and gain the edge you need over other applicants.

Before examining some specific job objective samples, let's discuss one more common problem with job objectives.

Avoiding "me" objectives and mushy career goals

The message has finally come across. Job objectives *are* important. Job hunters are finally taking them seriously, but what's this? Some job hunters got confused along the way and their job objectives have become flowery, wishy-washy, "me"-oriented statements that sound more like future career goals than current job objectives.

Don't confuse a job objective, which is a concrete, practical statement of what you are applying for now, with a futuristic, vague career goal as job hunters so often do.

Employers often see this:

JOB OBJECTIVE:

To obtain a responsible, challenging secretarial position with opportunity for advancement to a supervisory position.

Stick to the here and now. Avoid dreamy future aspirations, especially ones that focus on what you'd like to get out of the employer rather than what the employer can get out of you.

Here's another syrupy career goal that doesn't mean a thing to an employer:

JOB OBJECTIVE:

To find a career that is challenging, fulfilling, and allows for personal growth.

Again, this job objective focuses on *me's*: challenging for "me," fulfilling for "me," personal growth for "me." Even worse, this one doesn't even mention the actual position being applied for.

And this one's a real killer:

JOB OBJECTIVE:

To better myself and my family now and in the future. To have a job with security and stability.

Guess what's wrong with this one. Is there an actual position even mentioned here? No. And, again, it's totally a "me" (or in this case, a "me and my family") focus. There is nothing here to benefit the employer.

Writing your job objective

Now you can write your job objective. Remember, make it specific and clear. Don't think "me, me, me." Don't think "dreamy future career goal." Think "the exact job I'm applying for now," and if you're responding to a newspaper want ad, copy the position title exactly as written in the ad.

Here are some samples of specific job objectives to help you.

- A dental receptionist position.
- To work as a payroll clerk.
- An executive secretarial position.
- To work as a Legal Secretary/Estates Assistant.

You can also include the specific *work setting* being advertised (for example, in a bank, company, or corporation):

- Secretary for an ad agency.
- Position as a medical office assistant in a lab.
- Office administrator for a trust company.

You can use the *name* of the actual work setting:

- A receptionist position at J.D. Graphics.
- Word processing operator at YBX Incorporated.
- To work as a legal secretary at Whitman, Brown and Burney.

Or you can even include the exact *type of individual* for whom you wish to work:

- Administrative Assistant to a Corporate President.
- Secretarial position to a hospital administrator.

Supporting your specific job objective with resume content

Of course it's not enough to state that you want a certain position. Note that your resume will have to continually support your job objective by proving throughout that you have the necessary qualifications for that position. For instance, if "to work as an executive secretary" is your job objective, everything in your resume will have to focus intently on or play up as much as possible executive secretarial skills and duties over other ones. You will learn how to do that in the chapters coming up.

In conclusion

If you've made your Job Objective focused and clear and specific to the particular job you're applying for, you're already off to a strong start—in fact, you've just set the direction for the entire balance of your resume!

The Summary of Qualifications—Creating an Immediate Impact

Hook employers in the first few lines of your resume by giving them everything they want right from the start!

NAME
Address
City, State Zip Code
Phone Number

JOB OBJECTIVE

SUMMARY OF QUALIFICATIONS

FIGURE 2-5.

The Summary of Qualifications is a small paragraph that lists your most desirable qualities right at the top of the resume.

You have already given an employer a specific job objective so that she readily knows what you're after. Now give her a Summary of Qualifications so she won't have to search your resume for the most important skills and traits that she needs. Spell them out for her right off the bat!

First, we will discuss the basic method of setting up your Summary of Qualifications. Then we will delve into precise and unique tailoring techniques that are simple to create and invaluable to your resume success.

Setting up your Summary of Qualifications

There are many qualifications an employer looks for in a secretarial/clerical candidate, the most fundamental of them being:

- Dependability
- Experience
- Skills
- Personality

Basically, that is who you are, what you know how to do, and how long you've been doing it. Show an employer you have all the essential requirements and even outstanding skills in these areas through a carefully constructed Summary of Qualifications.

Under your Summary of Qualifications heading, get ready to use two or three lines. Use a scrap piece of paper for now, and hold off on forming your final answers until you've read this entire section.

Based on the four fundamental employer requirements, we're going to create your Summary of Qualifications. We'll do it by answering the first four questions that go through an employer's mind.

Dependability. Employer question #1: "Can I entrust my operation/ business to this person? Can I rely on him to be a completely responsible worker?"

It makes sense that an employer would worry about this first. A secretary, or any type of worker, for that matter, has to be dependable in order to be employable. If you had to hire a babysitter for your kids, a service to wash your windows, or a mechanic to fix your car, wouldn't their dependability be your first concern, too? Of course it would. This is probably the most basic requirement of all. Without it, everything else is worthless. Now, although just stating your dependability doesn't necessarily prove that you are, emphasizing it can help give an employer a secure feeling about you. There are several ways you can put this key point across. Choose the words that describe you best:

> dependable
>
> reliable
>
> responsible
>
> capable

So, to help ease an employer's dependability concern, a sample phrase to start off your Summary of Qualifications might read: "Highly dependable."

Experience. Employer question #2: "Has she ever worked at this type of job before?"

Most employers want to know that you've had some experience in the clerical field—that you didn't just fall off the turnip truck. Summarize the years of clerical experience you have.

Here your answer for your Summary of Qualifications might read: "Five years' secretarial experience."

Skills. Employer question #3: "Does he have the necessary skills to do the job?"

To answer this, you can choose from these categories of skills:

- Technical skills / Computer skills / Word processing skills
- Organizational skills
- Oral communication skills
- Written communication skills / English skills
- Public relations skills / People skills / Social skills / Interpersonal skills
- Typing or Keyboarding ability
- Dicta typing skills / Machine transcription skills
- Aptitude for math, figures, or numbers / Bookkeeping/ Accounting skills / Mathematical skills

I'll admit that the skills list is pretty long. You might ask, "How do I know which of these skills to include in my Summary of Qualifications?" The answer:

1. Pick your best or most outstanding skills. One or two are all you need to list. If you have trouble identifying your skills or wish to choose other or more detailed skills to include here, refer to Chapter 5, page 62, "Discovering Your Dynamic Skills" to help you.

2. Pick the most needed skills for the job:

   a) Look at your job objective. If it is geared toward a specific type of clerical position that may require one type of skill over another (for instance, a dicta typist requires typing or keyboarding ability, speed, and accuracy), emphasize those most needed skills in your Summary of Qualifications.

   b) Recall any job interviews you've been on. Think of the skills employers repeatedly ask for. For instance, computer skills are a vital requirement for today's office workers that all employers look for. Emphasize this or any other sought-after clerical skills in your Summary of Qualifications.

To satisfy the crucial skills question an employer asks, a sample answer for your Summary of Qualifications could be the following: "Excellent technical and organizational skills."

Personality. Employer question #4: What type of person is she? Is she easy to get along with? Will she create a good impression on clients/customers?"

An employer naturally wonders what type of person you are and if you have favorable traits for the job. Are you enthusiastic, dynamic, polite, respectful, supportive, eager to learn, considerate, energetic, cheerful, helpful, industrious, hardworking, or mature? There's a list even longer than this to choose from if you turn to Chapter 5, page 69, "The Characteristic Features List."

To give an employer a hint of your personality, your sample answer here could be: "Friendly and enthusiastic."

Assembling your Summary of Qualifications

Once you have chosen the skills you want to emphasize, indicated the amount of experience you have, stressed your dependability, and highlighted at least one good personality trait that will help you in your job, you have, in essence, answered the four fundamental questions an employer needs answered. Now, assemble your answers on your resume like this:

SUMMARY OF QUALIFICATIONS

Highly dependable. Five years' secretarial experience. Excellent technical and organizational skills. Friendly and enthusiastic.

There. Now you have an employer's attention. This mini-profile of yourself instantly satisfies his vital concerns while showing off some of your best assets.

Tailor It for a Perfect Job Fit—How to Match Your Skills to an Employer's Exact Needs

You can go a step beyond the Summary of Qualifications we have just created with one that is *precisely* tailored to the particular job you are applying for by zeroing in on the *exact* needs of the employer. For instance, instead of offering an employer "good computer, technical, or word processing skills," you offer "WordPerfect 6.0," the exact word processing skill needed. How do you do this? Easily—with the help of the newspaper want ad.

There is great pressure in the workplace nowadays to get results fast, and that means employers finding workers who have all the exact skills intact without the need for training.

When scouring the want ads, if you find that you have some or all of the exact skills a particular employer is looking for—fantastic! Shout it out as loudly as you can. Use a tailored Summary of Qualifications to show her you're it, she's found you, she doesn't need to look any further.

Recently, I placed a want ad for a medical secretarial position in a local newspaper. I clearly spelled out the five major requirements for the job: knowledge of WordPerfect 6.0, computer medical billing, excellent public relations skills, dedicated and hardworking, experienced and enthusiastic. Out of more than thirty responses I received, none of them specifically addressed these needs on their resumes. Sure, some lucked in and had a few skills scattered throughout their resumes that matched my list; but there was no deliberate effort to address or organize the particular requirements I specified. Time and again, job hunters fail to pick up on simple cues like these from ads. Why ignore the obvious? The biggest clue to what an employer wants to see sits right in front of you. Grab it and use it to your best advantage.

Setting up a tailored Summary of Qualifications

To tailor your Summary of Qualifications to an employer's exact needs, choose a newspaper want ad for a position you're interested in and analyze it. Here's how.

Let's say this was the ad you were responding to:

SECRETARY

We require a secretary with a mininum of two years' experience and strong organizational and communication skills. Competence in WordPerfect 6.0, dicta and keyboarding of 70+ w.p.m. are required.

Ask yourself what this employer specifically wants. Divide the requirements into the four categories by writing them out on a piece of paper like this:

Dependability	—is not specified
Experience	—minimum of two years required
Skills	—strong organizational and communication skills
	—competence in Wordperfect 6.0
	—dicta and keyboarding skills of 70 words per minute
Personality	—doesn't specify

Now, compare your own skills to the ones in the ad. If you have all or most of the skills the ad indicates, your Summary of Qualifications might read like the following:

Add dependability.

Use strong adjectives.

SUMMARY OF QUALIFICATIONS

Very reliable. Four years' secretarial experience. Excellent organizational and communication skills. Superb knowledge of WordPerfect 6.0 and 6.1. Accurate dicta typing skills of 85 w.p.m. Bright and conscientious.

More than the employer needs

Add personality.

Here you have given the employer the exact elements she's looking for and more—all in the first few lines of your resume. You couldn't be off to a better start than this!

Adding the power adjectives. Notice the use of adjectives such as "excellent" and "superb." Generally, in the Summary of

21

Qualifications, you should use the strongest words possible to convey an outstanding impression. However, be careful not to go overboard. Always evaluate your true self. Here's a guide to help you describe yourself most accurately while still creating a great impression.

If you have advanced skills, use adjectives like excellent, superb, exceptional, outstanding, and superior to make yourself shine, for example:

"exceptional people skills"

"superior communication skills"

If you have basic or average skills, use adjectives like good, accurate, and solid, for example:

"solid knowledge of medical terminology"

"accurate keyboarding skills"

If you feel that you're limited in a particular skill, you can still say "familiar with," "some knowledge of," or just "knowledge of." Any knowledge of or familiarity with a needed skill is better than none at all, for example:

"familiar with word processing"

"some knowledge of bookkeeping"

And if you're missing a required skill listed in the ad:

Option 1: Leave it out. Never claim to have skills that you don't. Instead, emphasize the features you do possess that match the employer's requirements.

Certainly, if you have already noted an exceptional skill in one area, it may balance out the lack of skill in another.

Option 2: Be vague rather than precise. (This is one place where general is better.) For example, say "good word processing skills" without specifying which ones you do or don't have.

Analyzing more want ads

Before creating your own tailored Summary of Qualifications, let's gain some more practice by analyzing various want ads.

JUNIOR SECRETARY

Busy downtown office currently offering opportunity for an energetic, highly motivated individual. WP 6.0 and completion of a recognized secretarial course required. Shorthand and creative writing skills an asset.

Again, ask yourself what this employer specifically wants. Divide the items into categories.

Education —Completion of a secretarial course (Here the employer is offering an opportunity to a new graduate. In this case, the educational requirement can take the place of experience or can be highlighted in addition to experience.)

Skills —WordPerfect 6.0 (required)

—creative writing skills (an asset)

—shorthand (an asset)

Personality —energetic

—highly motivated

Again, assuming you have these, your Summary of Qualifications could look like the following:

SUMMARY OF QUALIFICATIONS

Graduate of a two-year office administration course (achieving honor list status with a 4.0 G.P.A). Good knowledge of WP 6.0. Excellent English skills with flair for writing. Familiar with Forkner shorthand. Vibrant and extremely motivated.

Highlight education here because employer requires this.

Always include any outstanding achievements.

Here's another one:

RECEPTIONIST / SECRETARY

Fast-growing retail organization requires a reliable, hardworking individual with at least two years' secretarial experience. Good customer reception skills and telephone manners a must. Must be detail oriented and proficient in MS Word 6.0.

Dependability —requires a reliable individual

Experience —at least two years' secretarial experience

Skills —customer reception skills (a must)

—telephone manners (a must)

—proficiency in MS Word 6.0

Personality —hardworking

—detail-oriented

Thus, your Summary of Qualifications might read as:

Notice how a general skill is replacing a specific one here if you don't have the exact skill (of MS Word 6.0).

SUMMARY OF QUALIFICATIONS

Extremely reliable. Three years' secretarial/reception experience. Superb people skills and professional telephone manner. Thorough knowledge of word processing programs. Attentive to details. Efficient and hardworking.

And now for the last example:

EXECUTIVE SECRETARY / ADMINISTRATIVE ASSISTANT

A medium-sized west-end manufacturer seeks a well-organized, enthusiastic individual with a miniumum of 5 years' executive secretarial experience to provide secretarial and administrative support to the President in the day-to-day operations of the company. You are a mature, self-motivated professional with excellent interpersonal skills who can assume responsibility without requiring direct supervision. Your secretarial skills include WP 6.0, excellent keyboarding speed and accuracy, and a strong aptitude for figures.

Now, try to break this one down.

Dependability	—Can assume responsibility (without requiring direct supervision)
Experience	—Five years' executive secretarial experience
Skills	—WordPerfect 6.0
	—excellent keyboarding speed and accuracy
	—excellent interpersonal skills
	—well organized
	—strong aptitude for figures
Personality	—enthusiastic
	—self-motivated
	—mature

Presenting … the Summary of Qualifications for this job:

Always include outstanding professional secretarial credentials if you have them.

SUMMARY OF QUALIFICATIONS

Ten years' experience as a Certified Professional Secretary with seven of these as Executive Secretary to a Senior Vice President of a major bank. Exceptional office administration, organizational, and interpersonal skills. Excellent knowledge of WP 6.0. Keyboarding 100 w.p.m. Good mathematical skills. Responsible, energetic, and self-starter.

By now, you should be able to create your own tailored Summary of Qualifications effortlessly. But first, note the following tips.

Summary of Qualifications Do's and Don'ts

1. Don't copy the language of the ad word for word. If the employer requires "good public relations skills," you can convey this as "people skills" or "social skills." Be original. Use your own words and terms that convey the same meaning, as we did in the previous examples. If you need help in choosing your own wording, refer back to page 18 for the different skill categories you can use. And for help in choosing your own wording to describe your personality, refer again to Chapter 5, "The Characteristic Features List" section.

2. Don't list every single skill you have. The Summary of Qualifications is not the place for providing every skill or details of skills, for example, every computer program you've ever worked on. Here you focus on exact elements for the position. Later, in the Technical Skills and Special Abilities section of your resume (Chapter 5), you will give the employer more skills, details, and lots of them.

3. Do add any extra requirements that the employer specifies in the ad that are obviously important to her such as education or training (as we have done in the preceding examples).

4. Do add any outstanding academic or work achievements or accomplishments (as we have done in the preceding examples).

5. Do remember to support your claims throughout your resume. The rest of your resume must prove the claims you made in your Summary of Qualifications through detailed descriptions of your job duties, skills, and abilities (as you will learn to do in the chapters coming up and particularly in the section in Chapter 8 titled "Prove What You Say You Are—How to Back Up Your Summary of Qualifications Throughout Your Resume)."

6. Do be prepared to modify your resume for each different job. Your tailored Summary of Qualifications is exactly that—tailored! If you use this method, you'll need to modify your Summary of Qualifications for each job you apply for and you may have to alter or rearrange your supporting resume content a bit. (More on this in the section in Chapter 8 titled "How to Modify Your Tailored Resume to Fit Any Job Position.")

Beyond the Want Ads—Utilizing All Your Job Resources

As you have seen, newspaper want ads can be a great help in forming your Summary of Qualifications by showing you which skills and features to emphasize. However, it's important to note that there are many job sources other than want ads that you should not overlook. In fact, some jobs never even get advertised or posted at all because they are filled through different methods.

Among the many sources of job leads that you should actively pursue are:

- Employment or job information centers
- Personal contacts with friends, relatives, neighbors, and acquaintances
- Professional contacts with former employers, coworkers, colleagues, teachers, professors, instructors, and classmates
- School or college placement offices
- Yellow Pages
- Local businesses

Whichever source you use to locate an available position, always try to find out the most you possibly can about the position, so that you can match your skills to the employer's specific needs and effectively highlight them with a tailored Summary of Qualifications.

In Conclusion

You have learned how to analyze newspaper want ads, break down employers' needs into categories, and then address those needs by listing corresponding skills complete with powerful adjectives in your Summary of Qualifications.

With all this, you've certainly captured the employer's attention. It's time now to fully satisfy her. The Summary of Qualifications was just the appetizer. Time for the main course. On to your Job History—the meat of your resume.

3

Job History

Give Yours an Incredible Professional Polish

Your Job History is your most precious selling tool. It's proof that all the claims you made about yourself are true. It's where you don't just tell an employer you can do this or that, you show it—through specific descriptions of your previous jobs and responsibilities.

The Job History (Work History or Employment History) consists of four parts:

- Dates of employment
- Job titles and employer information
- Main function (sometimes)
- Job duties

In this chapter, we will explore these four parts. You will learn how to build powerful descriptions for all your job duties using a simple phrase-building formula and clerical examples as your guide. You'll learn to uncover your special achievements and how to describe them best. You'll learn to replace plain words with professional job language, and you'll learn to gather positive employer comments that add sparkle to your resume. Then you'll find out how to organize your job duties and positions in a way that tailors even your Job History to the job you're applying for. So, roll up your sleeves, and let's get to work.

NAME
Address
City, State Zip Code
Phone Number

JOB OBJECTIVE

SUMMARY OF QUALIFICATIONS

JOB HISTORY

19__ - 19__   **JOB TITLE**
                Employer, City, State

Main Function

- Job duties

FIGURE 3-1.

Dates of Employment and Position Titles— Handling the Nitty Gritties

Let's start with the Job History basics: your dates of employment, job titles, and employer information.

Dates of employment

These are the dates you began and ended your job positions.

JOB HISTORY

19__ - 19__

FIGURE 3-2.

You can either list the months along with the years:

March 1994 - September 1996

or you can list years only:

1994 - 1996

Either way is acceptable.

Job titles

These are the job titles for your previous jobs. You don't have to use the ones your previous employers gave you. Here's why:

Marla was hired five years ago as a clerk typist. As her department expanded, she took on numerous additional duties to the point that the responsibility of the entire office rested on her shoulders. Meanwhile, however, her official job title of clerk typist never reflected these changes because it was never updated.

You're free to create new titles for yourself if your jobs justifiably deserved them. Here are guidelines to help you decide what's right and wrong for you.

Avoid technical titles of particular companies or organizations such as:

Clerk Typist *III*

Secretary *Level V*

Junior Word Processing Operator

These are levels and numbers devised by a particular organization or workplace and hold valid meaning only for that workplace. Don't lock yourself into them.

Use specialty job titles (if appropriate):

Medical Secretary

Legal Secretary

Executive Secretary

These indicate specialized fields that require specialized knowledge. If you don't belong to any of these categories, it's perfectly fine to simply write "Secretary."

JOB HISTORY

19__ - 19__   **JOB TITLE**

FIGURE 3-3.

Or, here are some good titles that reflect today's new updated secretarial image. Choose the ones that describe you in your previous positions most accurately.

Administrative Assistant

Administrative Secretary

Administrative Coordinator

Administrative Specialist

Office Assistant

Office Supervisor

Office Manager

Office Administrator

Office Services Coordinator

Business Manager

Business Assistant

Executive Assistant

Be cautious, though. Make sure it's a reasonable title that your previous employer would agree with. The last thing you want is for a prospective employer to get contradicting information when following up on employer references.

Also, bear in mind the job position you're after now (that you stated in your job objective). If you're altering your job titles, try to make them relate as closely as possible to the job title you're applying for now. Of course, previous job titles that precisely match your job objective are best!

Employer information

Underneath your job title, type the name and address of the company or organization for which you worked, like this:

1994 - 1996   **<u>SECRETARY</u>**

DLM Design Studio, Beverly Hills, CA 10002

You don't need a full address. Leave out the street name to save space. It's perfectly acceptable this way.

The Main Function—Revealing the Full Scope of Your Job

The Main Function is a short introductory sentence that precedes your job duties. It summarizes the *basic role of your job* and indicates *for how many people you worked*. You need a Main

```
JOB HISTORY


19__ - 19__        JOB TITLE
                   Employer, City, State


Main function
```

FIGURE 3-4.

Function only when this information isn't already self-explanatory from the job title and employer information alone.

For instance, if your position title and employer information are:

SECRETARY

Low Weigh Clinic, Buffalo, New York

Prospective employers wouldn't know from this whether you worked for one boss or a staff of ten. In this case, you would need a Main Function.

To determine the Main Function of your job:

Ask Yourself:	*Sample Answer:*
What was the main role of my job?	- Performed secretarial duties
What kind of organization did I work in?	- Weight loss clinic
For whom did I work?	- 5 diet consultants and 2 nurses

Thus, your Main Function might read as:

Performed secretarial duties for a weight loss clinic comprised of 5 diet consultants and 2 nurses.

This secretary worked for seven people! This is important information an employer would never have known from the employer information and job title alone.

Let's try another one:

LEGAL SECRETARY

Zitman and Associates, Chicago, IL

Ask Yourself:	**Sample Answer:**
What was the main role of my job?	- Provided administrative and secretarial support and performed reception duties
What kind of organization did I work in?	- A general practice law firm
For whom did I work?	- Staff of 20 including senior lawyers, junior lawyers, and paralegals

Thus, a sample Main Function might read as:

Provided administrative and secretarial support to two senior attorneys and performed reception duties for the entire general practice law firm comprised of 20 lawyers.

Wow! Before listing a single duty, the employer already knows for what positions and how many people you were responsible. Now for all the job duties you list after this, an employer will understand the full scope of your job.

When do you *not* need to include a main function for your job position? When your job position and employer information look like this:

MEDICAL RECEPTIONIST

Dr. Kevin Wo and Dr. Sela Brody, Baltimore, MD

In this case, your employer listing and position title clearly sum it up. It's obvious that you worked as a medical receptionist for two doctors, with nothing much to be elaborated on. There's probably no need for a Main Function here.

So, analyze your employer listing carefully. If you think important information is not clear from it or if it alone doesn't do your position justice, by all means, include a Main Function.

Your Job Duties—Turn Weak Old Duties into Powerful Job Descriptions

After fourteen years as a secretary for a neurosurgeon, Joanne describes her work experience on her resume with this single phrase: "performed general clerical duties." Richard has seven years' experience as a senior office assistant and sums up his duties on his resume in these few words: "typed, filed, and answered phones."

JOB HISTORY

19__ - 19__   <u>JOB TITLE</u>
                Employer, City, State

Main function

- Job duties

FIGURE 3-5.

Despite the tremendous knowledge, experience, and specialized skills these individuals possess, they reduce their jobs to a most general level with dry, simplified descriptions of their duties, undervaluing themselves and decreasing their chances of landing a suitable job.

What a terrible waste of their true abilities and talents. A prospective employer will never know about them if they're not shown. These skeletal job duties barely touch on the essence of their work.

Don't fall into the same dead-end trap. Show the full range of your duties by firing them up with enthusiastic descriptions. Give details, and lots of them. Show everything you know, and describe everything you've done. Become a powerhouse at selling yourself.

How to form your job descriptions

First, break down that overused "general clerical duties" phrase into specifics. Starting with one of your previous job positions—preferably the most relevant one to the job you're applying for now—list all the job duties you've performed on a piece of scrap paper.

If this most relevant job position is also your most recent, fabulous! You can already begin to place it in reverse chronological order on the rough draft of your resume. However, if your most relevant job position is not a recent one, you'll probably need an alternative way to organize it. We'll discuss the organization of your job positions in more detail at the end of this chapter. For now, just start with your most relevant job and don't worry about its exact order.

Include all job duties—everything from basic to advanced. Don't worry about their order for now, either. These too will be organized at the end of this chapter.

To start you off, here's a list of common duties secretaries and office workers perform:

- Typed
- Answered phones
- Booked appointments
- Filed
- Received/greeted visitors
- Ordered supplies
- Took minutes
- Planned conventions
- Handled bookkeeping
- Entered computer data
- Wrote correspondence
- Filled out forms
- Trained other office workers

Notice that these duties are listed in their primitive form. Never enter them like this on your resume, as clerical workers so often do. They lack substance and sizzle. They're practically begging for an overhaul. Let's inject some life into them by giving them an incredible professional polish.

The Phrase-Building Formula

There's an easy method for enhancing your job duties and constructing your job descriptions; I call it the Phrase-Building Formula. With it, you build up each duty by asking yourself "What," "How," and "Who"—basically asking as many questions as you possibly can about each particular duty.

What? (What kind? What did you do?)

How? (How much? How many? How often?)

Who? (For whom, if the number of people is different from that indicated in the Main Function.)

On the following pages, we will transform each of the duties we have just listed into polished professional phrases. Keep in mind that the transformed phrases are general in nature. It's up to you to include the specific details that characterize your own job. Now let's go through the common duties you perform, dissect each one, and build new phrases using the "What, How, Who" phrase-building formula.

1. Typed

Practically every office worker knows how to type. The questions are what did you type, how much, and on what? Simply saying "typed" doesn't tell an employer much. It could mean you typed an odd memo and nothing more. If you typed so much that your fingers hurt—show it! Show the full range of your skills and experience by providing a detailed, accurate description.

Using our phrase-building formula, construct your job description now:

Ask Yourself:	Sample Answer:
What did I type? (List it all!)	- Letters, reports, documents, memos, invoices, lists
How much did I type?	- A lot
On what did I type?	- Electronic typewriter, word processor
What did I use?	- Dicta machine or handwritten notes

Thus your job description might read as:

Typed large volume of letters, reports, documents, memos, invoices, and lists using an electronic typewriter and word processor from machine dictation and handwritten copy.

Showing your full range of duties. Letters, reports, documents, memos, and lists all require different format styles. With this new job description, you're showing that you know them. You are also demonstrating your ability to operate a word processor, transcribe dicta tapes, and handle large volumes of work. These are a lot of important details displayed in our new, enhanced description.

Pleasing to the ear. Fiddle around with the order of the words until you get your new job description to sound just right. Reading it out loud can help you make sure the order of things you listed is pleasing to the ear.

Active, not passive. Use the active rather than the passive voice for more impact. For instance, we say "typed letters" and "answered phones," not "responsible for typing" or "phones were answered."

The specifics of *your* job. Include the specifics of your own job. For instance, if you've held a medical secretarial position, your "typing" job description should reflect it to look like this:

Typed *consultation* letters, *medicolegal* reports, *research* manuscripts, *case histories*, *inter-hospital* memos, and *patient* lists using a word processor and dictaphone.

Notice how the italicized words make this job description relate to the specific position.

Similarly, if you've held a legal secretarial position, a typing job description for you might look like this:

Typed and proofread letters and *legal* documents including *wills, deeds, affidavits,* and *briefs* from machine dictation, handwritten notes, and shorthand using word processors and electronic typewriters.

Starting to the get the idea? Let's continue now with transforming the rest of the job duties on our list.

2. Answered phones

You may say that answering phones is a straightforward task. Every secretary does it, and there's nothing more to be said about it. Wrong! Answering phones encompasses a wide range of skills and abilities.

Use the same phrase-building formula for constructing your job description:

Ask Yourself:	Sample Answer:
How many calls did I answer per day? (Emphasize this if it was a large amount.)	- 100 calls (or large volume or constant flow)
How did I handle the calls? (Did I just take messages or did I do anything more?)	- Took messages, transferred calls, dealt with inquiries
What kinds of calls or inquiries did I handle?	- Urgent matters, client problems, general questions

Thus, your job description might read as:

Answered 100 incoming calls per day; screened and transferred calls, relayed messages, and handled urgent matters, client concerns, and general inquiries.

What a difference! With the new polished version, an employer can actually picture you in the workplace setting, the phones ringing nonstop while you smoothly juggle the phone lines. Your hard work and abilities are starting to leap right off the page.

3. Booked appointments

Ask Yourself:	**Sample Answer:**
What kind of appointments?	- Meetings, client appointments, and conferences
What did it entail?	- Needed to coordinate them
For whom did I book them? (If this is different from the Main Function)	- For manager and eight staff members

Sample Job Description:

Booked and coordinated all meetings, client appointments, and conferences for manager and eight staff members.

4. Filed

Ask Yourself:	**Sample Answer:**
What did I file? (List it all.)	- Customer charts and business files
How much did I file? (Emphasize this if it was a lot.)	- 10,000 customer files (or a large volume)
What kind of filing system did I use? (Alphabetical, numerical, color-coded, or electronic?)	- Color-coded and numerical

Sample Job Description:

Filed and maintained 10,000 customer charts and business files using color-coded and numerical filing systems.

5. Received/greeted visitors

Ask Yourself:	**Sample Answer:**
Whom did I receive? (Emphasize this if it was a lot.)	- A lot of clients (or 50 clients per day)
What did it involve?	- Greeting visitors, recording client registration information, and preparing their files

Sample Job Description:

Handled busy client flow which included receiving and greeting visitors, recording registration information, and preparing client files.

6. Ordered supplies

Ask Yourself:	**Sample Answer:**
What did I order?	- Supplies, equipment, test materials
For whom did I order it?	- For whole department

Sample Job Description:

Ordered and maintained all supplies, equipment, and test materials for entire department.

7. Took minutes

Ask Yourself:	**Sample Answer:**
Where?	- At company board meetings
For whom?	- For boss
What did it entail?	- Reviewing, transcribing onto word processor
	- Results had to be short and accurate

Sample Job Description:

Recorded accurate and concise minutes for boss at special weekly company board meetings, and reviewed and transcribed notes onto word processor.

8. Planned conventions

Ask Yourself:	**Sample Answer:**
What did I plan?	- Biannual conventions and professional workshops
What did this involve?	- Preparing agendas, coordinating travel arrangements, and making hotel reservations
For whom?	- For 800 guests

Sample Job Description:

Planned biannual conventions and professional workshops; coordinated travel arrangements and hotel reservations for over 800 guests and developed and prepared workshop agendas.

9. Handled bookkeeping

Ask Yourself:

What did this include?

What did I use?

Sample Answer:

- Accounts receivable/payable, bank reconciliations, payroll, and monthly financial statements

- Manual and automated systems

Sample Job Description:

Handled bookkeeping—office accounts receivable/payable, bank reconciliations, payroll, and monthly financial statements—using manual and automated systems.

10. Entered computer data

Ask Yourself:

What did this include?

What kind of data?

Sample Answer:

- Storing and retrieving information on computer

- Customer and suppliers' accounts, personnel records, and statistical information

Sample Job Description:

Stored and retrieved computer data including customer and suppliers' accounts, personnel records, and statistical information.

11. Wrote correspondence

Ask Yourself:

What did this include?

What did I compose and edit?

Sample Answer:

- Composing and editing

- Correspondence and business reports for the president's signature

Sample Job Description:

Composed and edited correspondence and business reports for signature of the president.

12. Filled out forms

Ask Yourself:

What did I fill out?

Sample Answer:

- Requisitions, expense forms, petty cash vouchers, timesheets, absentee slips, and employee data sheets

Sample Job Description:

Completed various forms including requisitions, expense forms, petty cash vouchers, timesheets, absentee slips, and employee data sheets.

13. Trained other secretaries

Ask Yourself:

What did it include?

How many did I train?

Sample Answer:

- Supervising and evaluating them, teaching them all department procedures

- Three secretaries, junior level

Sample Job Description:

Supervised and evaluated junior secretarial staff of three which included training in all department procedures.

What a difference!

That's it for our list. What a difference these transformed job descriptions make! No longer are your duties two-worded, weak depictions of your job but rather solid, productive examples of your work that you can be proud of.

Writing your own job descriptions

These samples covered common secretarial and clerical duties. Don't copy them directly, but rather use them as your guide. Always include the specifics of your own job. Remember, every clerical position is different. There isn't just one way to describe your duties, but these are good typical examples you can learn from to create your own.

Spice Up the Simplest Clerical Tasks

Let's face it. As a clerical worker, you perform dozens of menial duties every day that are a part of your job and keep the office engine running. They aren't, however, grand achievements or glorious examples of your abilities. On your resume they tend to stand out as too simple.

But even the simplest, most mundane task may warrant a space on your resume if you spice it up correctly.

Take the following examples:

Picked up mail

Ask Yourself:

How much mail did I pick up?

For whom?

What did I do with the mail?

Sample Answer:

- A lot

- For whole department

- Separated it and gave it out to each person in the department

Thus, you could say:

Sorted and distributed large volumes of daily incoming mail to all department staff.

Stuffed envelopes

Ask Yourself:

What did this involve?

Sample Answer:

- Printing address labels, sealing and stamping envelopes

Sample Job Description:

Prepared correspondence for mailing, which included printing address labels and sealing and stamping envelopes.

There, that's better. These job duties may still be simple, but now, through an enhanced choice of wording, they too can convey positive examples of your work.

Adding the Human Touch

Besides showing your work duties and responsibilities, your resume should show your human side. How did you deal with visitors and coworkers? These descriptions will be your people skill provers and, because they're not as concrete or clear-cut as actual job duties, you might easily overlook them. For those of you who stated or emphasized in your Summary of Qualifications that you have good people, social, or public relations skills, it will be especially important for you to prove it here.

Here are some examples of "human touch" job descriptions or "people skill provers":

Established and maintained excellent relationships with clients.

Related well with clients, customers, suppliers, coworkers, and all levels of staff.

Calmed, comforted, and reassured injured patients and children requiring sutures.

Assisted customers with problems and eased their concerns.

Provided excellent customer service by attending to all customers' needs promptly and courteously.

Greeted visitors in a friendly and enthusiastic manner, answered any and all questions and concerns.

Developed good relationships with colleagues and coworkers, and helped create a pleasant office environment.

Any one of these would make an employer say "Hey, I could use a person like this!" They show that you are a caring person, that you understand the importance of fostering good relationships with everyone from a business sense and office environment sense, and that you go out of your way to represent the people you work for favorably; in other words, they show you are a true professional. Including a phrase like these gives your resume that added bonus that might very well make an employer pick you over others.

If you are or were like this, make sure to show it by including some human touch job descriptions of your own in your Job History.

Special Achievements—How to Find and Flaunt Them

Another way to capture the attention of a prospective employer is to show not only that you have effectively performed clerical duties and have good people skills, but also that you were instrumental in bringing about lasting positive results through special accomplishments or achievements.

Secretaries or office workers who have gone beyond their regular duties and taken the initiative to introduce positive changes or improvements into their jobs and into the organizations or companies they work for have, in essence, promoted themselves to a higher level—one that makes them hot commodities for prospective new employers. Emphasize these special achievements on your resume and it will likely get snapped up by an employer who will be more than eager to meet you.

Finding your special achievements

"What exactly is a special achievement and how do I know when I've contributed one?" you might ask.

A special achievement is anything that has produced lasting positive results, or any changes or improvements that have increased the production of a business or the efficiency of an office.

Ask yourself: "Have I ever thought up a new, different, or quicker way of doing something?" (For example, a better or more comfortable method of dealing with duties or situations.)

"Even if I haven't thought up anything new or better, did I tackle my work so thoroughly that the entire office ran more smoothly because of me, was ahead of schedule or more organized or efficient than before?" For instance, you might say to yourself "Actually, I did think up a new appointment scheduling system once. It saved me on mailings, and I also saved myself a lot of phone calls."

Let's use the phrase-building formula here, too. Only here, along with asking "What, How, and Who," ask "What was the *result*?" That is the key question to add to find your special achievements.

1. Made a new booking system

Ask Yourself:	*Sample Answer:*
What was the result of this new system?	- Fewer long-distance phone calls needed to be made
	- Fewer appointment cards needed to be mailed out

Thus, your special achievement might read as:

Devised and implemented a new recall appointment scheduling system which reduced long-distance calls and cut mailing costs by 20%.

(Include concrete figures or percentages if you know them.)

2. Made up newsletters and brochures

Ask Yourself:	*Sample Answer:*
What did this include?	- Company brochures and newsletters
What did you do with them?	- Mailed them to new and existing customers
What was the result of this?	- Gained new customers

Sample Special Achievement:

Initiated and produced marketing strategies such as company brochures and newsletters; mailed them to new and existing customers, thus increasing customer base by 30%.

3. Obtained billing information

Ask Yourself:	**Sample Answer:**
What did this entail?	- Contacted hundreds of patients and insurance companies for correct billing information
What was the result of this?	- Kept records and payment claims up to date, which increased monthly billing totals

Sample Special Achievement:

Contacted hundreds of patients and health insurance companies for outstanding billing information, thereby consistently updating records and payment claims and increasing monthly billing totals.

4. Started color-coded filing system

Ask Yourself:	**Sample Answer:**
What was the result of this?	- Could find files quicker and easier, and files didn't get lost or misplaced as often

Sample Special Achievement:

Introduced color-coded filing system which provided quick, efficient access and resulted in a decrease in lost or misplaced files.

5. Started new mailing method

Ask Yourself:	**Sample Answer:**
What was this new method?	- Using postage meters (instead of stamps) and lighter-weight envelopes
What was the result of this?	- Reduced mailing costs

Sample Special Achievement:

Implemented the use of postage meters and light-weight envelopes for mailing correspondence, which significantly reduced mailing costs.

6. Used a discount long-distance service

Ask Yourself:	**Sample Answer:**
What was the result of this?	- Reduced costs of long-distance calls

Sample Special Achievement:

Contracted with new discount long-distance companies which resulted in reduced long-distance bills.

7. Did extra leftover typing of other staff

Ask Yourself:

What was the result of this?

Sample Answer:

- Typing backlog would get cleared up

Sample Special Achievement:

Consistently cleared typing backlog of clerical staff.

Those were some solid examples of special achievements. Some of you may not even realize you have them. Think hard to find your own. Sometimes, what you might have thought was a simple work suggestion or improvement was actually a major results-producing accomplishment that you can now proudly display on your resume to thoroughly impress an employer.

Enhance It All with Positive Employer Comments

Positive employer comments can be a great addition to your resume. Whether it was a nice written evaluation about you or just a complimentary remark in passing, either of these can be added to your resume to give it life and individuality and further strengthen your candidacy.

For instance, if you have received a formal written evaluation praising your good work, add a comment or two from it to your Job History, for example, "Praised by manager as a devoted loyal worker." Even if you recall a supervisor or boss casually saying something nice about you such as, "You're the best secretary we've had—without you everything would fall apart," put it in your Job History (under an "Employer Comment" subheading). It can do wonders for your resume.

From Plain Words to Powerful Verbs—Your Key Word List

Of all the duties we've transformed on the previous pages, one thing they all had in common was the use of professional wording. We didn't just say we "looked after" things—we "maintained," "monitored," "coordinated," and "supervised." We didn't just say we "did" things—we "handled," "prepared," "organized," and "performed." Those are words that elevate tasks with their professional flavor.

Compare the following two paragraphs to discover the difference between plain language and professional job language.

Paragraph #1: plain language

I took care of many office duties. I helped my supervisor with travel arrangements. I wrote down statistics and put together my own reports. I did all the typing, gave out daily mail, and kept up an organized filing system. I watched over trainees in my department and even started up a training system whereby secretaries could learn new skills quicker and easier.

Paragraph #2: professional job language

I was responsible for many office duties. I assisted my supervisor with travel arrangements. I recorded statistics and compiled my own reports. I handled all the typing, distributed daily mail, and maintained an organized filing system. I supervised trainees in my department and even implemented a training system whereby secretaries could learn new skills more efficiently.

"Compiled," "distributed," and "implemented" instead of "put together," "gave out," and "started up." Which paragraph do you think would appeal to an employer more? Which has the sound of professionalism? Both paragraphs list identical duties but the first one uses plain words; the second paragraph replaces them with professional verbs that speak the language of a workplace setting and enhance your professional image.

Go through your job descriptions to see if any plain words have crept in. If so, you can polish them up now with the following word list—your guide to professional verbs.

Substituting plain words with professional verbs

Instead of plain words:	*Use professional verbs:*
did/ took care of	- performed - handled - managed - processed - completed - accomplished - operated - achieved

set up/ started up	- arranged - organized - established - initiated - implemented - introduced - launched - founded - invented - engineered - spearheaded
put together	- compiled - coordinated - collected - organized - arranged - assembled - accumulated - constructed
wrote	- composed - formulated - drafted
wrote down/ kept track	- recorded - monitored
kept up	- maintained
helped	- assisted - supported
watched over	- supervised - oversaw
led	- directed - headed - guided - conducted
made	- created - devised - designed - produced - established - invented - developed - formulated

made ready	- prepared
	- planned
	- arranged
made better	- improved
	- streamlined
	- revamped
	- revised
	- remodeled
	- restructured
	- revitalized
	- strengthened
	- upgraded
	- overhauled
	- transformed
made bigger	- expanded
	- enlarged
	- increased
checked or checked over	- reviewed
	- monitored
	- examined
	- inspected
	- verified
	- analyzed
made sure	- assured
	- ensured
gave	- provided
	- supplied
	- presented
gave out	- distributed
showed	- demonstrated
	- displayed
showed how	- instructed
filled out	- completed
got	- obtained
	- secured
	- acquired

Organizing Your Job Duties

Okay, so you have your job duties all enhanced and transformed into fabulous job descriptions. It's time now to organize them. We have to put them in some sort of logical order.

What do you think? Should the typing duty go first?... or maybe answering phones?... or how about booking appointments? Any of these may belong first or any of them may not, depending on which ones need to be emphasized.

It's really a matter of common sense. Certain job duties get first billing because they are more relevant or important than others.

The job duties that need the most elaboration and should be placed first or at the beginning of your list are:

- Job duties that are most relevant to the job you're applying for now. (This is the tailoring aspect at work again.) For example, if your Job Objective is a dicta typist position, you would place your typing or transcription job duty first or at the beginning of your Job History to emphasize early in your resume that you're right for the job and have had experience with the most crucial requirements of the job.

- Job duties that back up the skills you stated in your Summary of Qualifications. (More tailoring.) For instance, if you claimed that you have "excellent word processing skills" in your Summary of Qualifications, now's the time to prove it and emphasize it by including a word processing job description, elaborating on it as much as possible and placing it at the beginning of your Job History.

- Job duties that you performed best and that are impressive examples of your work.

- Job duties that you performed frequently and that were most important to the job.

The job duties that can go at the end of your list and don't need as much elaboration are:

- Job duties that are not as relevant or important to the position you're applying for now.

- Job duties that you didn't perform as well or that are not the best examples of your work.

- Job duties that were less important to your job or menial in nature. (You could probably eliminate these entirely to save resume space—unless, of course, these are relevant or important duties to the job you are applying for now.)

Group together special achievements

In addition, special achievements can be grouped together and placed at the end (or the beginning) of your Job History and set off with a Special Achievements heading.

Organizing Your Job Positions—Keep Tailoring Your Job History to the Job You're Applying for Now

Okay, we've done it all. Enhanced, transformed, organized, and tailored your job duties into powerful job descriptions complete with professional verbs, people skill provers, special achievements, and positive employer comments. But wait! We've done that for only one job. Now it's time to complete the whole process over again for each of your other job positions.

I know what you're thinking, "Oh, no, how many more?" Don't worry. You're going to detail only one to two job positions, or three at most! More than this would make your resume too long.

Relevant jobs only—the key to a winning resume

The one to three job positions you describe in detail should not necessarily be your most recent ones, but rather the most relevant ones to the job you're applying for now. Listing and providing details of irrelevant jobs is useless. It's only the relevant ones that matter. They are what make you a good match for the position you're applying for, and that's what tailoring your resume is all about.

The one to two (or three) job positions you should describe in detail are:

- Job positions that are the most relevant to the position you're applying for now.
- Job positions that are the most impressive examples of your skills and abilities (for the job you're applying for now).

If your relevant jobs are also your most recent, that's fabulous. Just place them in reverse chronological order in your Job History section, and they will naturally stand out at the beginning of your resume where they belong.

However, if your most relevant jobs aren't recent ones, it's not a good idea to use the chronological format. That's because the chronological format doesn't necessarily make you look good for the job you're applying for. It just blindly forces you to put your most recent jobs first regardless of how relevant or irrelevant they might be, and relevant or important jobs might end up buried at the bottom of your resume while totally unrelated ones take center stage. Thus, you need to find a way to emphasize these relevant jobs at the beginning of your Job History section. A slightly varying resume style called the Functional Style Resume is the answer. See Chapter 7, page 88, "The Functional Style Resume—Why It Can Overcome Almost Anything," and page 104, "Irrelevant Job Positions—When You Have Too Many or They're in the Wrong Place" for specific instructions on how to organize your job positions in this special style.

If you don't possess any relevant job experience at all because you are a career changer or a new grad, or if you're unsure how to organize your job positions because of any other special situations or problems, then you'll also need the special advice in Chapter 7. There you'll learn to tackle it all and still make yourself look your best.

In Conclusion

You did it. The hardest part—the crux of your resume—is formed. After this, you'll glide through the rest.

By now, you've created an exceptional Job History for your resume. Now it's time to provide some background on your formal training and education. Next up: the Education section of your resume.

4

Education and Training

How to Present Yours Best

I'll be honest. The Education section isn't quite as interesting as the other parts of your resume. Think about it: The Job Objective proclaims "I can meet the exact position you need filled." The Summary of Qualifications entices with "This is what I have to offer that you need," and the Job History boasts "These are the impressive duties I've performed and the experience I have acquired." But the Education section ... well, it is rarely more than a simple listing of your course titles and names of schools or training programs you have attended. Sort of an anticlimax. Nevertheless, it is still an important ingredient of your resume—one that shows an employer your commitment to grow and learn, and to develop your skills and business knowledge, and one that can help you reach your job goal.

Educational Credentials Can Help Support You for the Job You Want

Although education is not quite as valuable as your related work experience, it does play an important role in rounding out who you are on your resume. Ask yourself, "What did I do after my basic schooling that can positively contribute to the type of job I'm aiming for now?" Did you attend community college, business school, or other post-secondary institutions, or take any type of clerical or office administration courses? Even if you didn't take a formal secretarial training course, did you

NAME
Address
City, State Zip Code
Phone Number

JOB OBJECTIVE

SUMMARY OF QUALIFICATIONS

JOB HISTORY

19__-19__   JOB TITLE
                   Employer, City, State

- Job duties

EDUCATION

19__-19__   COURSE TITLE OR DIPLOMA
                   College or School, City, State

FIGURE 4-1.

take courses even somewhat related to your current job objective, and learn skills that you can now apply to an office job (for example, computers, English, mathematics, or communications)? Perhaps you've gone to college and have a degree or maybe your entire post-secondary education consists of a two-day computer workshop. That's fine. They're all valuable and need to be considered for inclusion in your resume.

There are three main elements about the Education section we need to discuss. They are what to include, what not to include, and where it all goes on your resume. Let's first deal with what to include.

What to Put In

Think back to all the courses or training programs you've ever taken or attended. Here are the ones most valuable for your resume.

Relevant courses are best

Certainly, relevant is always best and you should definitely list any courses or training programs that are directly related to a secretarial or office career. These might include:

- Formal secretarial, office administration, or clerical courses.
- Computer or data entry courses.
- Career-development workshops or seminars provided by your workplace or secretarial associations.
- Courses that are in any way related to the job you're applying for or in which you learned skills that can be useful to a clerical job (for instance, English, mathematics, accounting, business, economics, etc.).
- Any college or university degrees. Directly related or not, this is impressive higher education that should always be in your resume.

Unrelated courses—not great but better than none

Generally, you should omit courses that are totally unrelated to your current office job goal. However, if these are the only courses you've ever taken, it's probably a good idea to list them anyway. For example, let's say you're now looking for a secretarial position, but have spent two years taking an early childhood education course, which is the only post-secondary education you have. While this won't do much to support your current objective, it's better to show what you've done than risk the appearance that you have no post-secondary education at all. Don't emphasize or bold it as in a regular educational listing, but use a simpler rundown format. (See sample resume in Chapter 8, page 131 for an example of this type of low-key educational listing.)

What to Leave Out

You can't go too far wrong with your Education section, so you don't have to go crazy over what to leave out. Just use judgment and common sense.

Omit hobby-like courses

Always think of your image or the type of impression you'd like an employer to have of you. If you can't envision how a particular course will enhance your professional image, don't include it. For instance, makeup application courses, flower arranging classes, woodworking, or gourmet cooking are unrelated hobby-like courses that won't do anything to promote your professional or business image.

Scrap really old courses

If you've had a lot of new relevant training or working experience since some really old courses you've taken, then you might as well leave the old ones off. In this case, old courses will do nothing but reveal the fact that you've been around longer than you want an employer to know about.

High school—it's up to you

Generally, you don't need to include high school in your resume. The only time it might be necessary is if this was the highest education you have attained and you have nothing else to put in your Education section, or if you have received awards or honors or taken business/office courses in high school (these can add impressive information to your resume). Otherwise, high school is a given and you don't need to list it, especially if you've had a lot of working experience since then. It's really optional and completely up to you. Just be aware that if you're going to add high school to your educational listing, it's an immediate age giveaway.

So now you know what goes in your Education section. Time to tackle where the Education section appears on your resume.

Education or Job History—Which Comes First?

The most common mistake job hunters make with the Education section of their resumes is placing it before the Job History when it doesn't belong there.

The general rule—Job Experience before Education

When you have relevant working experience, your Job History takes priority over Education and is placed first on your resume. This makes sense because practical working experience is more valuable to an employer than any classroom training or instruction you may have received and should be emphasized first and foremost.

The exception to the rule—Education before Job Experience

There are some instances, however, when Education does take priority. Position your Education before your Job History if:

- You are a recent secretarial grad with absolutely no relevant work experience to focus on. (For in-depth instruction, see Chapter 7, page 99, "New Grads with Unrelated Work Experience or No Experience at All.")

- You have some related working experience, but your education or training is still more relevant or important to the job you're applying for now than any of the jobs you've held.

- You have exceptional relevant educational credentials (such as certification in your field) or outstanding academic achievements that you feel will catch an employer's attention if positioned before the Job History. However, as an alternative to placing the whole Education section first because of these credentials, you could just highlight them in your Summary of Qualifications instead.

Job retrainers—watch out

Today, more than ever, office workers are returning to the classroom and taking courses to upgrade and retrain themselves. They are out to gain new, updated, and specialized skills to survive and compete in this job market. So many new grads today are really job retrainers who already possess good, relevant working experience.

If this describes you, you might be tempted to display your brand new educational credentials first, as many job retrainers often do. But placing the emphasis on your Education section would only incorrectly make you look, at first glance, like an inexperienced new grad when you're not. Remember, working experience takes precedence over education. If you have relevant experience, show it first and show it fast. Then have your new training follow in the Education section as an extra bonus.

You can certainly show off those new, upgraded skills at the beginning of your resume in your Summary of Qualifications, too. (For detailed instructions on this, see Chapter 7, page 98, "New Grads with Relevant Working Experience.")

Now that you know what to include in the Education section and where to place it on your resume, let's form your education listing.

Forming Your Educational Listing

Always list your courses in reverse chronological order with your last or most recent ones first.

Here's how a typical Education section might look:

EDUCATION

1995-1996	**OFFICE ADMINISTRATION DIPLOMA PROGRAM**
	Careers Business College, Boston, MA
1991-1995	**SECONDARY SCHOOL GRADUATION DIPLOMA**
	Central High School, Boston, MA

Include the course title, name of school, city, and state. Bold, capitalize, and underline the course title rather than the school name.

If you've earned outstanding academic achievements such as honors or awards, add them to your listing and make sure to bold or italicize them so they stand out, like the following:

1995-1996	**OFFICE ADMINISTRATION DIPLOMA PROGRAM**
	Successful College, Detroit, MI
	Graduated with High Honors

If you possess certification in your field, don't forget to add this impressive information to your educational listing, as in the following example:

1996	**CERTIFIED PROFESSIONAL SECRETARY (CPS)**
	Professional Secretaries International, Kansas City, MO

If you'd like (and you have space), you can even place certification in its own section under a "Professional Development" heading.

Don't list course subjects

It's generally not necessary to list your course subjects, as many job hunters and especially new grads usually do. Education sections often look like this:

1994-1996   **SECRETARIAL CERTIFICATE PROGRAM**

Horizon's Business School, Oklahoma City

Course curriculum included:

- WordPerfect 6.0 (Advanced Level)

- Introductory Accounting

- Business Writing

- Office Computer Applications

- Machine Transcription

- Office Language Skills

- Office Procedures

- Records Management

Listing course subjects unnecessarily takes up valuable resume space. But that doesn't mean you should completely ignore them or let them go to waste, either. A good idea is to take these course subjects and list them as your skills instead (in your Technical Skills and Special Abilities section, coming up), because that's essentially what they have become—your valuable skills! (More on this in Chapter 5, page 67, "Use Your College Course Curriculum.")

In Conclusion

That's your educational listing. Make sure you take the time to consider what goes in it and what does not, highlight any outstanding academic achievements, and always be sure to place the Education section in the appropriate place on your resume—either before or after your Job History, depending on your situation. This is all you need to make Education another effective section added to your resume.

5

Technical Skills and Special Abilities

Dazzle an Employer with a Showcase of Your Skills

You've already given an employer most of what he or she needs, but it's not over yet. You're not finished showing the employer what you can do!

Remember the basic categories of skills you listed in your Summary of Qualifications? Well, there are details of those skills and dozens of other skills and abilities you possess that you want an employer to know about. These are displayed after your Education (or Job History) in a separate portion of your resume called "Technical Skills and Special Abilities"—a brief but action-packed section that literally showers an employer with every skill and feature you possess. It's the finishing touch with a bang!

Of course, your most outstanding skills or skills that are vital to the job you are applying for should always take their place at the beginning of your resume in the Summary of Qualifications rather than get tucked away in this later section of the resume. But here you can provide the details of those skills, and you may even find new, previously unrealized talents in this chapter that you might want to go back and insert into your Summary of Qualifications.

So, let's start forming your fabulous skills section. First up: Learn to recognize what your skills are.

Stop Taking Your Skills for Granted

Too often, secretaries and office workers take the many skills and abilities they possess for granted. You may have worked at

NAME
Address
City, State Zip Code
Phone Number

JOB OBJECTIVE

SUMMARY OF QUALIFICATIONS

JOB HISTORY

19__ - 19__   JOB TITLE
                   Employer, City, State

- Job duties

EDUCATION

19__ - 19__   COURSE TITLE OR DIPLOMA
                   College or School, City, State

TECHNICAL SKILLS AND SPECIAL ABILITIES

FIGURE 5-1.

a particular position for many years and never actually had to pinpoint the invaluable skills and knowledge gained on that job. Or, throughout different job positions, you might have acquired many wonderful new technical skills but perhaps never stopped to realize just how large this skills list had become. Even if you've already identified some of these skills and presented them on a resume, chances are the list you've come up with is not as comprehensive as it can be.

Consider this typical interaction with Sabrina, a resume client of mine. When we came to the Technical Skills and Special Abilities section of her resume, all she wrote down was "typing 65 w.p.m. and computer literate." When I asked her for other skills or details of skills, she didn't think she had much else to include.

I asked her, "What skills do you possess?"

Sabrina: Typing, and computers. That's about it.

Me: Okay, you know computers, what programs have you used?

Sabrina: WordPerfect 6.0.

Me: Was this the only program you've ever worked on?

Sabrina: No, there were some others, but it's been a while since I used them.

Me: That doesn't matter. What are they?

Sabrina: WordPerfect 5.1, Wordstar, and Volkswriter.

Me: Great, we'll list them all.

Then I asked her, "What other special skills do you have?"

Sabrina: That's really about it.

Me: Do you know how to dicta type?

Sabrina: Well, I did a bit of dicta typing but it was only for a really short time at this one job.

Me: That doesn't matter. It's still a skill you possess. We're going to put it in.

Me: What about bookkeeping or accounting? Are you familiar with that at all?

Sabrina: I took some bookkeeping in college, but I don't have great bookkeeping skills—just the basics. I don't know if I should include it.

Me: Of course you should include it! Having basic skills or not knowing something perfectly is not a problem, and shouldn't stop you from putting it on your resume. We'll just say "some bookkeeping" or "basic knowledge of bookkeeping."

And then somewhere along the conversation, it turned out that Sabrina was an English expert and had even helped many of her friends' kids with their school compositions and English homework.

Me: Wow, what a great ability to show an employer. Let's put it in—"Exceptional English skills"—we can even add "regularly tutor elementary and high school students on their written language skills."

Sabrina: You can put *that* in a resume? I never knew.

Sabrina's skills and abilities went from "typing and computers" (her initial response) to "WordPerfect 6.0 and 5.1,

Wordstar, Volkswriter, dicta typing, bookkeeping, and exceptional English skills." And we didn't stop there. We went on to find more.

You, too, probably have more skills than you think. Don't make excuses like "I'm not great at it" or "It was a long time ago" or "I thought it was obvious" or "I can't put *that* in my resume." On the contrary, you can and should include any and every detail that will help make your skills list become as full and vibrant as possible. Don't be afraid to sell all of your skills, qualities, and talents and to enhance yourself and your professional image to the maximum.

So get ready to think hard and dig deep. We will systematically find every skill you possess, draw out every feature, and note every tidbit of knowledge, be it a great command of the English language or the expert use of a computer. You will surely dazzle an employer and likely surprise yourself in the process!

Discovering Your Dynamic Skills

How do you pinpoint your own best strengths? To make it easy, let's break down all the skills and abilities you need to identify and present to an employer into the following three categories:

1. Technical skills

2. Special abilities or specialized knowledge

3. Characteristic features

We will go through each of these categories to find the strengths you possess in each. Then, at the end of this chapter, we'll put them all together to create your fabulous Technical Skills and Special Abilities section.

Let's begin.

You Have More Technical Skills Than You Think— How to Find and Use Them All

Technical skills are exactly what they sound like: They're all the skills associated with today's modern office technology—computers, equipment, machines, devices, and all the operating abilities associated with them.

You can easily identify your technical skills. You just have to jog your memory a bit, especially if you've been in the workforce a while. The key is not to take anything you've ever used or learned for granted.

To find your technical skills, you're going to recall and list all the computer software programs, office machines, equipment, and operating abilities you possess.

Computer software programs

Computer skills are vital for today's office jobs. Impress an employer with a complete rundown of yours.

On a piece of scrap paper, list the names of all the computer software programs you have ever used. Include word processing programs; accounting programs; database packages; communications, graphics, forms, and spreadsheet software; any program that you used on the job, learned in school, or taught yourself. In other words, include it all!

Your list of computer software programs might look like the following:

- WordPerfect 6.0 & 6.1
- Microsoft Word 5.1 & 6.0
- Lotus 1-2-3 Version 5
- dBase IV and V
- AccPac Plus
- AmiPro Version 3.1

Office machines and equipment

If you've worked in an office in the last few years, you've undoubtedly become familiar with a large range of office machines and equipment that most office workers simply take for granted. Just start recalling all the machines and equipment you have ever used and you'll see how quickly you gather an impressive list.

Your equipment list might include the following:

- computers
- electronic typewriters
- laser printers
- inkjet, dot-matrix, or daisywheel printers
- transcription equipment or machine dictation equipment
- fax machines

- teletype machines
- scanners
- modems
- electronic memory telephones
- cellular telephones
- answering machines
- photocopiers
- electronic mail-handling machines
- electronic card readers
- calculators
- etc.

You can add the brand names to any of these if you wish. For instance:

- IBM, Apple, or Wang computers
- Hewlett-Packard laser printer
- Canon photocopier
- Etc.

Operating abilities

Now list any operating abilities you have associated with the computers or equipment listed above.

Your operating abilities might include:

- keyboarding 75 w.p.m.
- dicta typing or machine transcription skills
- desktop publishing
- spreadsheet preparation
- graphics
- etc.

Heed the minimum typing speed. The minimum typing/keyboarding requirement for most jobs and for secretarial course completion is 50 to 55 w.p.m. (words per minute). Don't list a typing speed below 50 words per minute. It will hinder rather than help you. If your typing speed isn't at least up to this, try emphasizing accuracy instead of speed. For instance, you can always write, "accurate typing or keyboarding abilities" and still look good.

Listing it all

If you found yourself digging up equipment and skills you thought were obvious and never dreamed of listing on your resume—good. That's the idea. You're supposed to kick up a storm. List it all.

From a while back? Don't be afraid to list things you've used or done even several jobs ago. It doesn't matter if you haven't recently utilized these skills or if you've only utilized them for a short period of time. They're still part of your collection of skills and you're going to list them all.

Not perfect at it? Even if you're rusty or don't have a perfect handle on it, that's okay too. When you feel you're limited at a particular skill, don't disregard it entirely or be afraid to include it on your resume. It would be a shame to have even these skills go to waste. As long as you have some familiarity with it, include it. All you have to do is indicate to what degree you're competent at that skill. For instance:

Add:	*To get, for example:*
Some	- "some AccPac Plus"
Some knowledge of	- "some knowledge of dBase IV"
Basic knowledge of	- "basic knowledge of Lotus"
Some experience with	- "some experience with transcription equipment"
Some familiarity with	- "some familiarity with Windows software"

Here, you're saying, "I may not be an expert at it, but I've still had some valuable experience with it." By adding these, you're not misleading anyone and you still get to make your resume's technical skills list as comprehensive as possible.

Your technical skills—how they look so far

By now, you have all of your technical skills listed on pieces of scrap paper. Start putting them together in the Technical Skills and Special Abilities section of your resume and you'll get something that looks like the following:

TECHNICAL SKILLS AND SPECIAL ABILITIES

WordPerfect 6.1, Microsoft Word 5.1 & 6.0, Lotus 1-2-3, dBase IV and V, AccPac Plus, AmiPro, keyboarding 75 w.p.m., dicta typing, computers, electronic typewriters, laser printers, fax machines, teletype machines, scanners, modems, answering machines, and photocopiers.

| still need special abilities |
| still need characteristic features |

{

{

See how this section is shaping up? Computer programs, office equipment, and operating abilities together make up a large array of your technical skills, past and present. And don't worry if your own list isn't this long; even a fraction of it will impress. Remember, you've only just begun to form your Technical Skills and Special Abilities section; we still need to identify and add two more categories of skills—your special abilities and characteristic features. Let's go on to those now.

Your Fabulous Special Abilities—Learn How to Identify Them

Special abilities (or specialized knowledge) are the special talents you possess, specific knowledge you've acquired, or particular methods or procedures you've become familiar with. Finding these skills is also quite clear and straightforward. As with technical skills, it's just a matter of tracing back to everything you've ever known or done.

To find your special abilities or specialized knowledge, recall and list on a piece of scrap paper any and all special talents, knowledge, or abilities you may have.

Here's a sample list to help you:

- good English skills
- aptitude for figures
- legal or medical terminology
- shorthand 100 w.p.m.
- minute taking
- bookkeeping (manual and automated)
- proofreading
- editing
- researching

- report writing
- speech writing
- public speaking
- etc.

How can you easily identify your own special abilities? Here are three tips to guide you:

1. Recall your best subjects in school

Think back to your school days (elementary and high school). Recall what you were always good at. What were your best subjects or the subjects you were naturally drawn to? Was it English? Or maybe math? Some people are naturally better at certain subjects than others. Just because something comes naturally or easily to you doesn't mean you should overlook it. Recognize where your natural talents lie so you can use them now to sell yourself. For instance, if you've always been good with numbers, then say so. Mathematical abilities are more than handy for any office job and will make you a more valuable candidate. Make sure an employer knows it by listing it as one of your special abilities on your resume. You can say "aptitude for figures," "numerically inclined," "good with numbers," or "excellent accounting skills."

Or perhaps you hated math, but English was a breeze for you. Language skills, written and oral, are crucial for your office job and are another example of a wonderful special ability to include if you have it. "Excellent command of English language," "good English skills," or "strong written communication skills" are all different ways of expressing your proficiency in this area.

So think back to what you were always good at, recognize any natural talents you may have, and use them to further enrich your resume and promote yourself.

2. Use your college course curriculum

Recall the courses you took in secretarial school or community college. You'll find that you can use some of the *actual titles* of your course subjects as your special abilities. For instance, if your curriculum included subjects entitled "Legal Terminology I," "Introductory Business Writing," and "Pitman Shorthand," these are not just course titles anymore. These have all now essentially become skills you possess and they can be listed as such. Thus, you could say that "legal terminology," "business writing," and "Pitman shorthand" are your special abilities or specialized knowledge. Instead of listing these as course subjects in your Education section, present them here as actual skills. It's more impressive that way.

3. Recall abilities acquired on the job

Think about the previous jobs you've held. What new methods, procedures, or abilities have you picked up that can be useful for another office job? Perhaps you've become familiar with a certain type of bookkeeping, for example, "familiar with One-Write Bookkeeping System"; or perhaps you've developed good research abilities on the job, and can now claim that you have "excellent research skills"; or you might have learned how to write reports or give presentations, and thus can now say that you're an "excellent report writer" or "good public speaker." So try to include any and every type of special ability you've acquired on the job, and you'll see that they'll be more than helpful in landing your next one.

Adding languages

If you speak several languages, here's one good place to mention that. You can add them to your Special Abilities or, if you'd rather and you have the space, you can put them in a separate Languages section of your resume, which you will learn how to create in Chapter 6, "The End Sections."

Your special abilities—how they look so far

Once you have identified and gathered all of your special abilities, add them to your technical skills to look like the following:

TECHNICAL SKILLS AND SPECIAL ABILITIES

WordPerfect 6.1, Microsoft Word 5.1 & 6.0, Lotus 1-2-3, dBase IV and V, AccPac Plus, AmiPro, keyboarding 75 w.p.m., dicta typing, computers, electronic typewriters, laser printers, fax machines, teletype machines, scanners, modems, answering machines, and photocopiers. **Good English skills, aptitude for figures, shorthand 100 w.p.m., minute taking, bookkeeping, report writing, public speaking, proofreading, editing, researching.**

still need characteristic features

Talk about showering an employer with your skills! Your list might not be as long as this one; it doesn't have to be. Even if you can think of only one or two special abilities, that's great!

You can either lump everything together the way we did on the previous page or, if you have a lot, you might want to divide and organize them with subheadings as you will learn how to do a little later on. But first, on to the last category of skills we need to identify and add—your characteristic features.

Finding Your Characteristic Features

Characteristic features make up who you are. They are the distinctive qualities and traits you have within you, the personality strengths you possess. Technical skills and special abilities tell an employer what you know and what you can do. Characteristic features are just as important because they can tell an employer what kind of person you are and what you'd be like on the job.

Are you organized, thoughtful, energetic, detail-oriented, trustworthy, efficient, flexible, or self-motivated? Never really thought about it? Well, now's the time to accurately identify your traits and features. How? With the Characteristic Features List—a comprehensive word list and mini-evaluation that can simply and quickly help you describe yourself. Here we go.

The characteristic features list

Below and on the following pages is a large selection of descriptive words or characteristic features. Your job is to choose the ones that sound the most like you.

Circle the words that you feel describe you best (not more than one word per group):	The corresponding statements can help you decide if it's really you:
punctual prompt	I always come to work or school on time.
friendly outgoing sociable pleasant	I enjoy interacting with people and always treat everyone warmly.
helpful supportive	I always try of be of assistance to anyone who needs it.
dependable responsible	My employer can always count on me for everything he or she needs.
reliable capable competent	

loyal committed dedicated devoted	I genuinely care about doing a good job for the organization or people I work for.
honest trustworthy sincere	I never cover up mistakes, and can be entrusted with all aspects of an office/business.
thorough precise accurate detail-oriented meticulous	I proofread my own work and always work at something until it is perfect.
fast worker efficient productive	I am able to meet deadlines and use my time well to really get things done.
conscientious diligent hardworking industrious	I put a real effort into doing the best work I possibly can.
progress-minded goal-oriented achievement-oriented	I work toward getting results from whatever I do.
team worker team player cooperative	I work well with others.
neat orderly organized	My work space is tidy, and I always know where to find what I need.
eager to learn willing to learn	I'm open to learning new things and like to take on different types of work.
self-motivated self-starter self-disciplined	I have incentive to do my work even without supervision or direction from others.
fast learner bright intelligent sharp	I can easily pick up new skills and tasks.

innovative inventive creative	I am good at devising new or better ways of doing things.
energetic enthusiastic vibrant dynamic	I have a zest for living and tackle my work with a high level of energy.
respectful courteous polite	I always display good manners to everyone.
flexible adaptable versatile	I can handle change well and can easily fit into any situation.

Narrow it down to your best three

Once you have circled all the words that describe you, write them out on a piece of scrap paper so you can review them. You'll likely have gathered a fair-sized list of characteristic features. But you're not going to put *all* of them in your resume. You don't want to bombard an employer with too many characteristic features, or they'll lose their effectiveness. That's why you're going to narrow it down. Two or three is all you really need, that is, two or three of your absolute best.

You feel that all the words you've chosen describe you well, but which are the most compelling features about you or describe you best of all? Once you have decided which those are, you can put them together like this:

dedicated, organized, and hardworking

Make sure it's an impression you want

Look at the three words you chose. How do they look and sound together? Do they create an image you're comfortable with and one that you'd like to present to an employer? If not, go back to the word list you've come up with and choose a different combination of words that might satisfy you better, or you can even go back to the words you circled in the Characteristic Features List and replace any of them with their synonyms that you feel sound better or suit you better. The key is to make sure that not only do the *individual* words you choose reflect you well, but also that the combination of these words creates an impression you want and one that you'd most like an employer to have of you.

Don't duplicate your Summary of Qualifications

Keep in mind the personality strengths you put in your Summary of Qualifications. Make sure the characteristic features you use here are not exactly the same ones you have already listed there. If you find you have unwittingly selected the same words that are in your Summary of Qualifications, go back to your word list and choose some of your other features instead.

Adding the power adverbs

Add extra power to your characteristic features by using adverbs to strengthen and enliven them. For instance, "thorough" can become "extremely thorough," "organized" can become "well organized" or "very organized."

Here are some power adverbs you can add to any of the words you've chosen.

Add:	To get, for example:
Extremely	- "extremely conscientious"
Highly	- "highly capable"
Very	- "very progress-minded"
Exceptionally	- "exceptionally fast learner"

As always, honestly assess yourself to make sure you're justified in using these. Don't just add them to sound good; use them only if they accurately portray you. And don't overdo it by adding adverbs to all three characteristic features. One or two of these is more than enough.

Putting It All Together—Beat the Competition in One Fell Swoop

Now that you've pinpointed your best characteristic features, it's time to put everything together—yes, all of it, from the beginning of this chapter until now—your technical skills, special abilities, and characteristic features in one convincing display.

All together now, here's how it looks:

TECHNICAL SKILLS AND SPECIAL ABILITIES

WordPerfect 6.1, Microsoft Word 5.1 & 6.0, Lotus 1-2-3, dBase IV and V, AccPac Plus, AmiPro, keyboarding 75 w.p.m., dicta typing, computers, electronic typewriters, laser printers, fax machines, teletype machines, scanners, modems, answering machines, and photocopiers. Good English skills, aptitude for figures, shorthand 100 w.p.m., minute taking, bookkeeping, report writing, public speaking, proofreading, editing, and researching. Dedicated, organized, and hardworking.

There you have it. Your storehouse of skills, abilities, and features—to knock the socks off any employer. The skills just keep coming, at full speed, one after another. It's everything you have to offer—in one fell swoop!

All in one paragraph or break it down into subsections

In the example above, everything is lumped together in one big paragraph. This is fine, and you can follow the same layout for your own resume. However, don't be afraid to organize things differently if you wish.

If you've gathered a lot of skills, you might want to break down your skills paragraph into subsections and add subheadings or introductory phrases, as in the following example:

TECHNICAL SKILLS AND SPECIAL ABILITIES

Extensive knowledge of computer programs:
- WordPerfect 6.1, Microsoft Word 5.1 & 6.0, Lotus 1-2-3, dBase IV and V, AccPac Plus, and AmiPro.

Operate a wide range of office equipment:
- IBM and Apple computers, electronic typewriters, Hewlett-Packard laser printers, fax machines, teletype machines, electronic mail-handling machines, scanners, modems, and photocopiers.

Abilities also include:
- Keyboarding 75 w.p.m., shorthand 100 w.p.m., dicta typing, bookkeeping, minute taking, report writing, public speaking, proofreading, editing, and researching.
- Good English skills and an aptitude for figures.
- Very organized and extremely thorough.

This type of layout will give your Technical Skills and Special Abilities section a clearer, more organized look, but note that it will also take up more space in your resume, which you must decide if you can afford. Remember, you are striving to keep your resume to one page. You'll be better able to decide which layout works best for you after you've viewed the sample resumes in Chapter 8 and once you've begun your final printed draft, when you can determine the exact spacing of your resume.

Popular or up-to-date technical skills first

Surely, you've worked hard to gather everything you know to include in your skills section. However, use common sense when deciding on the order for placing your technical skills.

The technical skills you should position first or at the beginning of your listing are:

- technical skills that are most recent or up-to-date (such as the latest computer software).
- technical skills that are most popular in the workplace or the most widely used today (such as a word processing program that most organizations seem to be using).

Stay on Top—Keeping Up with the Hottest Skills of Today and Tomorrow

You couldn't have presented your skills and abilities more powerfully in your resume. That's wonderful. However, keep your eyes open to what goes on around you in the job world. Always be aware of the current skills and features employers look for and make sure to include and emphasize them on your resume if you have them, or go out and work at getting them if you don't. This is the way smart job hunters stay on top of the job hunt.

Stay informed

The first step in keeping up with hot skills is knowing what they are. You can find "now" skills or what employers are particularly looking for at any given time by:

- Regularly analyzing newspaper want ads.
- Joining secretarial or professional associations in your field. (More on this in Chapter 6, the section headed "Memberships.")
- Reading career-related magazines, newsletters, and updates.
- Reading the business/careers section of your local newspaper.

Stay current—upgrade and retrain

Once you know what the latest skills are, stay a step ahead of the competition. Be a dynamo—go out and get them:

- Attend career-related professional development workshops and seminars.
- Enroll in community college courses and continuing education programs.
- Upgrade your computer skills by taking a computer course, and get a home computer if you don't already have one so you can practice, practice, practice.

- If you're currently working, accept technical change in the workplace. Don't be reluctant to learn that new program—instead plunge into it enthusiastically. Consider it your invaluable on-the-job training that can be added to your collection of skills to make your resume a more effective one and yourself a stronger candidate.

In Conclusion

You've learned to identify your skills, abilities, strengths, and talents and how to effectively present all of them in your resume and do a knockout job of selling yourself. Fantastic! You're in the final stretch of your resume preparation. On to the end sections—the very last bit of your resume.

6

The End Sections

Hang in There, You're Almost Done

You've formed every crucial resume part. Time to wrap it up with the end sections of your resume—the last and easiest ones to produce.

In this chapter, you will learn about the optional Languages and Memberships sections, you'll learn how to handle and present your References, and you'll also find out what kinds of outdated information should always stay out of the resume. So let's finish it up now!

Languages—Optional but Valuable

Languages are simply the foreign languages that you can speak, read, write, or understand. Although including them in your resume is optional, it's usually a good idea to list them if you know them. They might just make you a more valuable candidate for the position.

Take the case of Amanda, a new secretarial graduate and resume client of mine who had been looking for a job for nine months with no success and barely any offers for job interviews. One day, we polished up her resume according to the instructions in this book and also added her languages. Within about a week, an employer who was looking for someone with precisely her foreign language skills (to effectively communicate with the organization's non-English-speaking clients) asked her for a job interview and ultimately offered her the job. You never know which particular element of your resume will strike just the right chord to get you noticed or make you more appealing—even languages can do it.

```
                            NAME
                           Address
                      City, State Zip Code
                        Phone Number
  _____

  JOB OBJECTIVE


  SUMMARY OF QUALIFICATIONS


  JOB HISTORY

  19__-19__        JOB TITLE
                   Employer, City, State


  - Job duties



  EDUCATION

  19__-19__        COURSE TITLE OR DIPLOMA
                   College or School, City, State



  TECHNICAL SKILLS AND SPECIAL ABILITIES

  LANGUAGES
```

FIGURE 6-1.

So, definitely include any foreign language skills you possess that you know are a particular requirement for the position, and even include them if you believe there's any chance at all they might be a helpful asset in the job you're applying for.

You can put your languages here in a separate Languages section or you can list them back in your Technical Skills and Special Abilities. It's up to you. Either way is fine.

Listing your languages

The Languages section is short and simple. Here's a sample of how it might look:

LANGUAGES

Fluent in Spanish and Italian

You can also express your language skills in any of the following different ways:

Speak Russian

Speak and write Italian

Oral and written knowledge of French

And even if you don't have written skills or aren't fluent, you can still write:

Understand Polish

Semifluent in Greek

Can communicate in Chinese

Memberships—That Little Extra That Can Mean a Lot

Memberships are the associations or organizations you belong to. There is an association for practically everything these days. From the International Chain Saw Wood Sculptors Association to the National Organization of Mall Walkers, there's a group out there for everyone, but saying you're a member of any of these will do nothing for your resume except take it off track.

Don't bother with irrelevant or hobby-like associations and steer clear of religious or political ones. The only associations that add any real worth to your resume are the professional ones in your field. Always ask yourself, "What type of membership or association can enhance my professional or business image?" The answer: Professional secretarial associations always do.

Professional associations and what they can do for your resume

Professional secretarial associations are the leaders of your profession. They provide resource materials for their members such as newsletters, periodicals, and publications. They hold meetings, offer development programs, and generally keep members up to date on the secretarial profession and office world.

Indicating that you belong to one can show an employer that you have an interest in your career, that you are committed to a standard of excellence, and that you are actively keeping abreast of rapidly changing office procedures and technology. And if you happen to hold any type of leadership role within the association, even better—that immediately says you possess positive qualities such as leadership and organizational abilities.

NAME
Address
City, State Zip Code
Phone Number

JOB OBJECTIVE

SUMMARY OF QUALIFICATIONS

JOB HISTORY

19__ - 19__   <u>JOB TITLE</u>
Employer, City, State

- Job duties

EDUCATION

19__ - 19__   <u>COURSE TITLE OR DIPLOMA</u>
College or School, City, State

TECHNICAL SKILLS AND SPECIAL ABILITIES

LANGUAGES

MEMBERSHIPS

FIGURE 6-2.

Thus, a simple membership listing can reveal a host of positive things about you. If you are affiliated with or are a member of any type of professional secretarial association, include it in your resume.

Listing your memberships

Here is what your Memberships listing might look like:

MEMBERSHIPS

Professional Secretaries International
National Association of Executive Secretaries

Addresses aren't necessary. Just list the name of the association, and titles you hold, if any, with your city or division.

If you don't already belong to a professional association in your field, consider joining. Refer to the "Appendix—Your Guide To Professional Associations," for a listing of major professional secretarial associations around the world.

If space allows

Before adding a Memberships or Languages section to your resume, consider how much space you have left. Ideally, your resume should not exceed one page, and by now you are likely on the last inch or centimeter of your resume. (Of course, you will be better able to gauge this once you're in your final draft.) Remember, Memberships and Languages are optional sections. Carefully consider whether to put them in if they're going to make your resume go on to a second page, and certainly don't cram them onto an already too-full first page. Take comfort in the fact that your most important resume parts are already there. If there's adequate space for these additional sections, great, but if they make your resume go on to a second page when otherwise it wouldn't have, decide carefully whether they're worth adding. (Or don't give up just yet—for advice on how to trim your resume to fit things onto one page, see the section in Chapter 9 on "Tips for Saving Resume Space.")

Leave Out the Outdated for a Stronger, More Focused Resume

Just as it is important to put certain things in your resume, so it is important to leave others out.

At about this point in the resume, job hunters used to add all kinds of personal data and irrelevant hobbies and interests. That was the style a while ago, but it's now outdated. The problem is that some people haven't stopped doing it.

Scrap personal data

Weight, height, general health, marital status, and number of children were common resume features. This section used to look like this:

PERSONAL DATA

Birthdate: Feb. 24, 1965

Marital Status: Single

Height: 5'5" Weight: 125 lbs.

Health: Excellent

Never include these items in your resume! Not only is it outdated, making you look as if you haven't kept up with simple basic resume styles, but it is discriminatory for an employer to base a hiring decision on any of these factors, or even to ask for the information.

Forget hobbies and interests

This is a section that keeps popping up on resumes rather frequently considering that it too is totally outdated. Hobbies and interests seem to be a harder habit to break.

Skiing, swimming, dancing, cycling, skating, aerobics, windsurfing, diving, camping, sculpting, painting, piano, photography, modeling, classical music, needlepoint, tennis, movies, interior decorating ... I could go on and on. The variety of hobbies and interests that job hunters used to list on their resumes is staggering.

The reason for including these in the first place was the well-rounded person theory. Job hunters believed that the more they showed employers how multifaceted they were, the stronger a candidate they would make. But not only are these irrelevant hobbies and interests totally useless to an employer and unnecessary for your resume, they can even backfire on you.

When a resume is overloaded with hobbies, interests, and activities, it can make an employer question whether the job applicant will be fully dedicated to the job. The one interest employers care about is your interest in doing a good job for them. Anything that deters you from that can be viewed negatively. For instance, an applicant who stressed on her resume that she loves recreational travel only raised red flags in an employer's mind. "Will she take off from work frequently to travel?" or "Would she really prefer a job that involved more travel? " were among the unsettling questions stirred up.

So say good-bye to hobbies and interests, on your resume that is, and you'll soon find that keeping all irrelevant and outdated information out will make your resume a stronger and more focused one.

References—What They Are and How to Use Them

The References section is the one you'll probably like best of all. That's because it consists of four words or fewer:

"References Available Upon Request"

or

"Attached"

Period. Nothing more. Now you're finished. Hooray!

But wait! Your References section might be finished just by adding these words, but we need to discuss the actual references—what they are, who you get them from, and how you present them to an employer.

NAME
Address
City, State Zip Code
Phone Number

JOB OBJECTIVE

SUMMARY OF QUALIFICATIONS

JOB HISTORY

19__ - 19__   <u>JOB TITLE</u>
Employer, City, State

- Job duties

EDUCATION

19__ - 19__   <u>COURSE TITLE OR DIPLOMA</u>
College or School, City, State

TECHNICAL SKILLS AND SPECIAL ABILITIES

REFERENCES

FIGURE 6-3.

What is a reference?

A reference is an endorsement or recommendation. It is someone backing you up, giving you approval, supporting you for
employment. Generally, you need to provide three references.
You prepare these separately from your resume (they're either a
list of names of people to contact or letters of reference or
both), and you usually hand them over to an employer at the
job interview.

Who should you get your references from?

References from previous employers are ideal, teachers or
course directors are the next best, and in a jam even your doctor or lawyer might do.

1. Previous employers. The best and most acceptable references are from previous employers. Ideally, you should provide
employer references from the positions detailed in your resume.
If you can't provide at least one, it will look fishy. Managers, directors, supervisors, or anyone for whom you directly worked
are included in this category. If you can't get satisfactory references from any previous employers for whatever reason, or can't
get all three that you need, then go to the next option.

2. Teachers, professors, instructors, and course directors.
References from teachers or instructors (preferably from relevant courses you've taken such as office, secretarial, or business
programs) are the next best type of reference. That's because
teachers can comment on many of the same things an employer
would. They can vouch for your work habits, your academic capabilities, and your skill level, and they may be familiar with
your personal attributes. New grads with no working experience will especially need to use them.

    If you can't provide employer references or teacher refer-
ences, as a last resort, you can use the next option.

3. Your doctor, lawyer, or accountant. Any person in a professional or prominent position who knows you well could probably pass as an acceptable reference. Although these people can't
claim to know what you'd be like on a job or what your technical
or academic capabilities are, they can provide character references. They can vouch for your positive character traits and give
some insight into your personal background. But, remember,
they're a last resort—use them only if you have no other choice.

Friends and family—the big no-no. Never use friends or family as references (unless that friend or family member happened to be your employer). It is totally unprofessional and unacceptable. What prospective employer cares about what your best friend has to say about you, and would any employer seriously consider the opinion of your brother-in-law? You'd be surprised how many secretarial job applicants submit reference lists comprised of family and friends. Don't do it. It will only make you look desperate and hurt your chances rather than help you.

How do you present your references?

References come in two forms. One is the verbal reference or phone reference, such that you supply an employer with a printed list of names to contact. The other is the written reference or letter of recommendation that you have obtained for precisely this purpose.

Phone references. You should provide at least two, preferably three, references neatly typed on a sheet of paper. Do not attach this sheet to your resume, but do have it ready to hand over to an employer at the job interview. Make sure the people on your list have given you permission to use their names, and you must be extremely confident that the people you have chosen as your references will provide an excellent appraisal of you or at least a satisfactory one.

Your reference sheet should look like the one shown in Fig. 6-4.

Include the person's name, title, name of company or organization, address, area code, and phone number. Also, make sure your own name, address, and phone number are on the top of the reference page, so a busy employer will know to whom they belong.

Reference letters or letters of recommendation. As important as phone references are, don't make the mistake of relying on them alone. If you know a certain employer will give you an excellent reference, by all means, get it in writing, in the form of a reference letter or letter of recommendation.

Don't assume your previous employer will be at that particular company or organization forever. Employers get replaced or retire, companies and organizations move or go out of business, and then you may face the task of playing detective to try to locate them. The most glowing reference that you

> **Mary Smith**
> **123 Main Street**
> **Montgomery, AL 10002**
>
>
> **REFERENCES**
>
>
> **Mr. Nolan Bassett, President**
> Compu-world Inc.
> 62 Manswood Ave, Unit #14
> Birmingham, AL 10002
> (123) 555-4366
>
>
> **Frances Sanders**
> Director, Office Administration Program
> Horizons Business College
> 450 Carter Road
> Birmingham, AL 10002
> (123) 555-7818
>
>
> **Erica Peterson, Manager**
> Heritage Realty
> 1605 Golden Beach Drive
> Tampa, FL 10002
> (123) 555-3799

FIGURE 6-4.

were counting on can suddenly become lost for good. Why take that chance? Obtain reference letters or letters of recommendation from as many employers as you can, preferably before you leave your job while your good qualities and valuable work are still fresh in the employer's mind. Collect these letters of reference, and build a reference file for your job hunting arsenal.

You can hand an employer copies of your best reference letters along with a phone reference list at the job interview (an employer will likely still want phone references, so have them ready), or better yet, send any truly excellent reference letter you might have right along with your resume.

Excellent Reference Letters—If You've Got Them, Flaunt Them!

If you have an excellent or exceptional reference letter, don't wait to use it. Send it along with your resume package. Why hide a document that proves how great you are? Do everything in your power to increase your chances—get it in front of the employer to encourage him or her to want to meet you. It can serve as an instant backup to what you've claimed in your resume. It's immediate proof right in the employer's hands that you are what you say you are.

Do note, however, that while it can be a good idea to send along a reference letter, it's not exactly standard practice, so make sure not to turn your resume from a one-page document into a thick pile of sheets. Keep it to one token letter only. Don't attach it, just include it, and make sure it's worth going against the grain—your letter should be something that will make an employer say, "Wow."

In Conclusion

You did it! All the parts of your resume are formed. The rough draft of your resume is complete. Pat yourself on the back for a job well done. However, before you print it up in its final form, we're going to take some time to address those job hunters with special resume needs. If you're a new grad, career changer, an overqualified individual, or an individual reentering the workforce, you're going to need the special advice coming up in Chapter 7.

Even if you don't belong to any of these special categories, you still can't afford to skip the next chapter. You may very likely have other common resume problems such as employment gaps, short-term jobs, or too many irrelevant jobs, and the next chapter will show you how to handle them all. Chapter 7 provides interesting tips and tricks that can help make your resume as powerful as anyone else's and also includes instructions on the Functional Style Resume—a special resume style that expertly camouflages any shortcomings you may have. So stay tuned; special advice for all kinds of special situations is up next.

7

New Grads, Career Changers, and All Types of Special Situations

How to Conquer Your Resume Problems and Beat the Competition

Few job hunters have perfect work histories. Most people possess all kinds of problems, big and small.

You might be a new grad worried about a lack of experience. Or perhaps you're a career changer agonizing over a lack of relevant work experience and skills for the job. If you're an individual reentering the workforce (especially after a lengthy absence), you fear appearing outdated, lacking new technical skills, and looking as if you haven't done any work in years.

If you possess any other common resume problems that plague job hunters—such as employment gaps (periods of time when you've been unemployed), short-term job positions (that make you look like a job hopper), irrelevant job positions (too many or in the wrong place, that make you look like an unlikely match for the job), being overqualified (the appearance that you're going down in job level instead of up)—you're equally worried that these blemishes will stick out sorely on your resume and hold you back from landing interviews and jobs.

You're justified in thinking like this. "How," you ask yourself, "can my resume compete under these circumstances?" Don't despair. Now, even your special situation needn't disqualify you, and your so-called resume problems can be fixed for good.

Dispel Your Worries

It's time to dispel all your worries because things are much better than you think. Fortunately, there are many tips and advice you can gain from this chapter to help you look just as good as anyone else, or even better. There's even a special resume style that can do wonders for you. Its called the Functional Style Resume and it's the solution you've been waiting for.

So before we tackle the distinctive problems of each special situation, let's first discuss the basics of the Functional Style Resume so that you'll understand exactly what it is and why it can be the answer for so many different types of problems.

The Functional Style Resume—Why It Can Overcome Almost Anything

The Functional Style Resume gives you enormous freedom. It allows you to organize your Job History any way you want, or more precisely, any way that will make you look best for the job you're applying for. That's why it is so effective. You're not bound by any precise chronological order of job dates or even by any precise previous job titles. You are free to organize your previous work experience in a new and innovative way that covers your shortcomings and makes you look your best.

How does it work?

A Functional Style Resume is not an entirely different thing. Don't think that this is a totally new resume with brand-new rules. It isn't. All we're going to do is take everything you've learned up until now about resumes and use the same basic principles to create a slightly different version. In fact, all the parts of the chronological resume—the Job Objective, Summary of Qualifications, Education, Technical Skills and Special Abilities—are exactly the same in the Functional Style Resume. It's only your Job History that gets a new look.

The Job History—Functional Style

First take a look at what a Functional Style Resume basically looks like. (See Fig. 7-1.)

NAME
Address
City, State Zip Code
(Area Code) Phone Number

JOB OBJECTIVE:

SUMMARY OF QUALIFICATIONS:

RELEVANT EXPERIENCE:

Job Title or Functional Heading:

-
-
-

Job Title or Functional Heading:

-
-
-

TECHNICAL SKILLS & SPECIAL ABILITIES:

EMPLOYMENT HISTORY:

Date   Job Title, Employer, City
Date   Job Title, Employer, City
Date   Job Title, Employer, City

EDUCATION & TRAINING:

Date   Course Title, College, City
Date   Course Title, College, City

REFERENCES:

Available upon request or Attached

Job History becomes Relevant Experience. → (points to RELEVANT EXPERIENCE)

Quick rundown of job positions, employers, and dates → (points to EMPLOYMENT HISTORY)

FIGURE 7-1. Basic resume format—Functional Style.

Notice that the Job History section is now titled Relevant Experience and gets formed a little differently. It can be formed in either of two ways:

Method 1—by using job titles only, without any dates, or

Method 2—by replacing job titles with new functional headings.

Method 1—job titles without any dates. You can omit all of your job dates and list your previous job positions in whatever order is best for your resume. Here's how it might look:

RELEVANT EXPERIENCE

<u>**AS AN ADMINISTRATIVE ASSISTANT**</u>:

-

-

<u>**AS A CUSTOMER RELATIONS MANAGER**</u>:

-

-

<u>**AS A DICTA TYPIST**</u>:

-

-

This method allows you to place your most relevant positions first, regardless of how far down the road they might have been. This effectively tailors your resume to the position and makes you appear to be a good match for the job. This method is especially useful for:

- Job hunters whose most relevant positions are not their most recent ones.
- Job hunters with irrelevant positions interspersed among relevant ones.

Also, by omitting dates in this section of the resume, you are forcing the emphasis directly onto your experience, duties, and accomplishments rather than on any dates that might reveal negative things about you. Thus, this method is also useful for anyone needing to camouflage problem dates such as:

- Individuals reentering the workforce.
- Job hunters with employment gaps.
- Job hunters with many short-term jobs.

Method 2—replacing job titles with new functional headings.
A second, more daring way to organize your Job History in the
functional style is not only to omit all of your job dates but
also all of your previous job titles. Instead, you'll group together relevant duties by category under new functional headings, as in the following example:

RELEVANT EXPERIENCE

<u>OFFICE SUPPORT:</u>

-

-

<u>PUBLIC RELATIONS:</u>

-

-

<u>ACCOUNTING EXPERIENCE:</u>

-

-

This method allows you to make an otherwise irrelevant
Job History look relevant to the job you're applying for.

Pulling out office or clerical type duties from irrelevant
jobs, grouping them into categories, and giving them new relevant headings is an innovative way to create a job experience
section that makes you look like a good match for the job.

This method is especially useful for anyone without directly related work experience, such as:

- Career changers
- New grads (sometimes)

or for anyone whose job titles don't quite complement the type
of job they're seeking now, such as:

- Overqualifieds (sometimes)

Of course, here too, dates won't show up because they are
omitted from this section of the resume. Therefore, this method is
equally useful for anyone needing to camouflage problem dates.

Dates are revealed at the bottom of your resume

You must note, however, that with either of these methods,
your job dates will eventually be revealed at the bottom of

your resume in a section entitled Employment History. This section provides a quick rundown of all the things you left out of your functional work experience section, namely dates, titles, and employer information. Here's an example of what it looks like:

EMPLOYMENT HISTORY

1995-1996 **SECRETARY,** Neil's Carpet Sales, San Jose

1994-1995 **RECEPTIONIST,** Woodward's Designs, San Jose

1992-1993 **OFFICE CLERK,** Gulligan's, Oakland

It's important to include this section because if there aren't any dates at all, employers will view you suspiciously. Now, I know what you're thinking. You're probably asking yourself, "What do I gain with the Functional Style Job History if an employer ends up seeing my problem dates and titles after all?"

The answer: The Functional Style Resume eliminates dates from the important Experience section of your resume to give an employer a chance to gain interest in you and see your best strengths and most relevant features first. The hope is that by the time the employer reaches the dates and titles at the very bottom of your resume, he or she will already be sold on you or at least have an interest in you, and any problem dates or irrelevant job titles will matter very little or not at all.

On to solving your resume problems

Now that you've been introduced to the Functional Style Resume and have a basic idea of how it works, it's time to see what it can do for you. Let's delve into each special situation or particular problem you may have.

Career Changers—From "Unlikely Candidate" to "Good Match for the Job"

You're a career changer. You want a secretarial or clerical position but you've had experience only with unrelated type jobs (and you haven't necessarily had any formal relevant training either). How on earth, you ask yourself, can your resume compete with that of someone already experienced in the field?

The problem

Your biggest problem is undoubtedly the fact that your past job experience is totally unrelated to your current job goal. In a traditional chronological format, here's what your resume might look like:

JOB OBJECTIVE: A Secretarial Position

JOB HISTORY:

1996-Present **WAITRESS**

Johnny's Deli, Savannah, GA

- Served tables.

- Took phone orders.

- Helped customers select menu items.

- Opened and closed restaurant.

1992-1996 **CASHIER**

Supermart, Augusta, GA

- Served customers.

- Rang up sales on cash register.

- Helped bag groceries.

- Assisted with store maintenance.

You have to admit that if this was your resume, you wouldn't be looking like a great match for the job. Sure, your Job Objective states that you now want a secretarial position, but there's nothing to back it up. Instead, your Job History brings your resume down by shifting the focus away from your goal.

Too often, career changers have no idea how to make themselves look like a match for the job they want. They mistakenly assume that just by stating their new job goal, an employer will magically figure out that they are suitable for the position, or that an employer will ask, "Hmm, is there anything in here that matches the position I'm offering and can contribute to my needs?" But it certainly doesn't work that way. All an employer will see is an applicant with a bunch of unrelated jobs and no experience in the position he or she is applying for, and in five seconds the resume will go into the "no" pile or the garbage.

The solution

You must find a way to create a relevant work experience section. Here's how:

1. Dig up clerical or transferable duties.

2. Group them into categories under new functional headings (using the Functional Style Job History—Method 2).

1. Dig up clerical or transferable duties. Analyze yourself and your previous jobs. Pull out and emphasize any clerical or administrative duties, and make a rough list of them. Right now, you're probably saying, "What clerical duties? I've never performed any!" Well, it simply isn't so.

Often, clerical duties such as bookkeeping, administrative work, public relations, etc. are hidden or unrecognized parts of many different types of jobs. Dig them up and use them. For instance, if you were an interior decorator, don't focus on the irrelevant aspects of the job such as your flair for choosing and coordinating colors; focus instead on experiences and achievements that can be valuable or transferable to your new office job goal.

Perhaps you could relate that you assisted customers and suppliers and handled all their needs and concerns (these would be your customer or public relations skills), or that you calculated prices (these would show your mathematical abilities), that you handled paperwork, phoned in orders (this would be your office or administrative experience)—all useful and valuable abilities for any office job.

Similarly, if you were a shoe salesperson, don't focus on the types of shoes you sold or how you designed store window displays. Think of all the things that can be adapted to your new office job goal. These again might be assisting the public, handling monies, being responsible for cash and receipts, operating a computer, or whatever else you can think of. Do this for any job, and you'll be surprised at all the office-related or clerical type things you come up with.

2. Group them together under functional headings. Once you've formed your list of clerical type duties, group them into categories, and give them new appropriate headings to replace your old irrelevant job titles. To help you, here's a list of sample headings you can choose from:

- Public Relations / Customer Service / Public Contact / Client Contact

- Office Support / Office Administration / Office Management / Administrative Experience

- Clerical Experience / Reception Experience

- Business Management / Business Experience / Management Experience
- Planning and Coordinating / Scheduling and Organizing / Organizational Experience
- Bookkeeping / Accounting Experience / Financial Experience

Following the above advice will give you a new, improved Work Experience section that sells you in a whole new way. For example, let's have another look at the Work Experience section of the Waitress/Cashier job applicant. This time, we've pulled out her clerical/transferable duties and grouped them under new functional headings. Now all her experience is properly revised to adapt to her new office job goal.

JOB OBJECTIVE: A Secretarial Position

RELEVANT EXPERIENCE:

CUSTOMER RELATIONS:

Provided excellent customer service to thousands of customers:

- Promptly and efficiently tended to all needs.

- Patiently dealt with inquiries and concerns and effectively resolved problems.

- Boosted repeat business and attracted new customers by regularly providing fast, friendly service.

ADMINISTRATIVE EXPERIENCE:

- Answered 50 incoming calls per day; accurately recorded phone orders.

- Processed orders and bills using computerized system.

- Maintained records of sales, and prepared daily customer reports.

- Balanced books and made deposits.

Yes, believe it or not, this *is* the same applicant. Instead of "served tables," or "helped customers select menu items," we eliminated the irrelevant waitress aspect and got transferable duties like "provided excellent customer service to thousands of customers ... etc."

What a difference. She now looks as if she's had appropriate experience and is all geared up for an office job. So, Career Changers, forget about your irrelevant job titles and duties. For you, functional style job histories are definitely the way to go!

Dig up hidden clerical activities from your daily life. If you have trouble finding clerical duties or enough clerical duties from within your jobs, look at your daily life.

People do all sorts of clerical-related work or activities as part of their daily living without even realizing it. Anyone who writes checks, pays bills, and does their own banking, plans vacations, fills out forms or documents, schedules carpooling, operates a home computer, heads a club or organization, or helps out a family member or friend with their business, is in essence already familiar with the basics of office or clerical work. There are many life tasks you perform that can rightfully take a place on your resume.

Just don't say "Planned a vacation for me, my spouse, and the kids to Florida this winter and got the cheapest price I could find." Professionalize it by saying: "Coordinated all travel plans—purchased airline tickets, reserved accommodations, and utilized special discounts at peak travel season."

Add special points to your Summary of Qualifications. Focus every part of your resume, not just your Job History, to your new office job goal. Here are some tips to help make your Summary of Qualifications relate to your new clerical objective.

1. Find and emphasize skills and features valuable to an office job, especially ones required for the particular job you're applying for.

2. Try to make up for your lack of experience in the field—add a line or two stating your commitment to developing your new career and/or your willingness to learn. You might try something like the following:

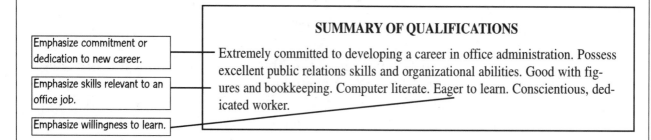

Emphasize commitment or dedication to new career.

Emphasize skills relevant to an office job.

Emphasize willingness to learn.

SUMMARY OF QUALIFICATIONS

Extremely committed to developing a career in office administration. Possess excellent public relations skills and organizational abilities. Good with figures and bookkeeping. Computer literate. Eager to learn. Conscientious, dedicated worker.

3. You can also add a line that sums up your work experience in a new, innovative way. For instance, you might not be able to say "Ten years of secretarial experience" but perhaps you can say this true but equally powerful statement: "Ten years' experience assisting clients or customers."

4. In addition, stress how adaptable or versatile you are (that is, only if you really are, of course) to show that you can easily handle a career change.

Join the computer revolution (if you haven't already). Try to find as many office-related technical skills as you can to place in your Technical Skills and Special Abilities section. (See the instructions in Chapter 5 to help you find yours.) If you're missing crucial ones for an office job, such as computers, it probably means it's time you joined the world of automation and took a computer course. It will make a world of difference to your job finding success!

If you follow the above instructions, even as a career changer, you'll have a better than good chance to leap over the competition and get what you want. Your new innovative resume can do it for you!

For a before and after sample resume of a career changer, see pages 158 to 160.

New Grads—From "Inexperienced Novice" to "Good Solid Candidate"

Believe it or not, there are some positive things about being a new grad, fresh out of school and embarking on your first work or office work experience. And there are employers who recognize the advantages.

First of all, you likely haven't yet formed any particular method or style of doing things, so an employer can train or mold you to a particular company style. Also, employers recognize that new grads are usually energetic, willing to learn, eager to prove themselves, and likely to work hard to carve a place for themselves in the working world. Last, but perhaps most importantly, coming straight out of business school or community college, you are likely to possess the latest, up-to-date technical skills and computer knowledge.

However, on the downside, employers are justifiably concerned about your lack of experience (or lack of relevant experience) and possibly even a lack of self-confidence. Therefore, you have to find ways to put yourself on top.

As a new grad, the most important thing you can do is change an employer's reaction to your resume from "Oh, an inexperienced new grad" to "Fabulous, a good candidate for the job!" How do you do this? To find out, let's divide new grads into two categories—those with relevant working experience (who are really job retrainers) and those with unrelated work experience or no working experience at all.

New grads with relevant working experience

You're a new secretarial or office course graduate. You already have some relevant office experience, but you can't wait to place your shiny new educational credentials *first* on your resume and top it off with a listing of all the great new course subjects you studied. You're sure this new training of yours will really impress an employer.

Not so fast!

The problem

Your resume at first glance spells "inexperienced new grad" when you're not. Practically the first thing an employer sees is this:

EDUCATION:

ADMINISTRATIVE ASSISTANT DIPLOMA PROGRAM

Successful Business College

Courses included:

- Computer applications (Lotus and dBase)

- Business writing

- Records management

- Introductory bookkeeping

- English and communications

Don't get me wrong: This training is impressive. However, nothing quite beats experience, and if you place your Education before your Job History, you're selling yourself short by saying: "This is the most important thing I have to offer," when it's not.

The solution

Position Job History before Education, turn course subjects into skills, and add special points to your Summary of Qualifications.

Position Job History before Education. Place your relevant working experience or Job History first, before the Education section of your resume (as discussed in Chapter 4, "Education and Training").

Once you've had relevant working experience, no matter how far down the road it was or how short the duration—even a placement job from your course will do—you've joined the ranks of working secretaries and your resume should reflect that.

Use a chronological format. You'll probably be fine with a chronological format for your Job History, that is, if you don't have problem dates, recent unrelated jobs, or other shortcomings. If you have these problems or others, then see the appropriate instructions for your particular situation coming up.

Turn course subjects into skills. As we've discussed in Chapters 4 and 5, it's not necessary to list course subjects in your Education section. It's better to give yourself a more effective Technical Skills and Special Abilities section and list your course subjects there as skills.

Add special points to your Summary of Qualifications. It's a good idea to mention your new education and training and newly acquired technical skills in your Summary of Qualifications, but remember, stress the fact that you have experience—first!—as in the following example:

Emphasize experience first.
Mention your new skills or recent training.

SUMMARY OF QUALIFICATIONS

Experienced Data Entry Clerk. Newly upgraded computer skills—honors grad of an office skills program. . .

For a before and after sample resume of a New Grad with relevant working experience, see pages 155 to 157.

New grads with unrelated work experience or no experience at all

You're a new secretarial or office course graduate. You're armed with everything you need to approach the workforce. You can't wait to get out there and begin your job search.

The problem

Your resume reveals that you have no experience, or no *relevant* working experience. An employer is reluctant to take a chance on you—it's impossible to know if you have what it takes to handle the job.

The solution

Show them you do have what it takes by emphasizing the right things on your resume. Position your crucial Education before your irrelevant Job History and use innovative techniques to try to turn that Job History into relevant working experience.

Position Education before Job History. Focus on your education and training, as this is most relevant and important for the job you're applying for. Position it first, before any irrelevant Job History you may have. (Here, you can either add course subjects to emphasize your Education or, again, if you wish, list them as skills instead.)

Turn your Job History into relevant working experience. Do what a Career Changer would do for your Job History—use the Functional Style Format, Method 2, to create a relevant work experience section.

Analyze your previous jobs, pull out and group together as many clerical related duties as possible, add new relevant functional headings, and voilà, you've created a work experience section that shows you're familiar with basic clerical duties after all. (Refer back to "Career Changers," page 92, for detailed instructions on this.)

If you have no working experience whatsoever, two words are your guide: Dig deep! Really deep—to odd jobs, summer camp, volunteer work, etc. You can even find those hidden clerical activities in your daily life to group together and place on your resume. (Again, see the Career Changers section for instructions.)

Add special points to your Summary of Qualifications. To try to compensate for your lack of experience or relevant experience, here are some special points you can add to your Summary of Qualifications:

1. Emphasize your education and training, any honors or awards you may have received, and your newly acquired computer or technical skills.
2. Include a line stating your willingness or eagerness to train or learn.
3. Add a line stating your commitment to developing your new career in your chosen field.

For instance, your Summary of Qualifications might read as:

Emphasize commitment to building new career.	**SUMMARY OF QUALIFICATIONS**
Show off your newly acquired skills.	Extremely dedicated to building a career in office administration. Honors graduate of a two-year office administration program. Up to date with latest word processing and computer software programs. Highly dependable, enthusiastic, and very eager to learn.
Emphasize willingness (or eagerness) to learn.	

Of course, don't forget to focus on any specific requirements or features an employer is particularly looking for.

Follow the above tips and advice, and even as a new grad, you'll be successful in reaching your job goal.

Individuals Reentering the Workforce—How to Avoid Looking Outdated

You were a secretary. You were responsible for hundreds of appointments, greeting and meeting clients, organizing your employer's schedule, maintaining financial records, solving dilemmas, and utilizing all of your skills and abilities. You were your employer's right hand and could be relied upon to handle every aspect of the office professionally and efficiently. Sounds great. What's the problem? The problem is that was in 1977.

For whatever reason, you've been out of the workforce and you're sure those nonworking years will show up like a huge empty chunk on your resume, branding you as "unemployable."

To top it off, while you've been gone, the office world has dramatically changed. It has undergone huge technological advances. Computers, modems, fax machines, and E-mail are scary terms indeed. You feel lacking and possibly even obsolete.

The problem

You have a large time gap on your resume where you look as if you haven't done anything. An employer also is likely to assume your skills and knowledge are out of date. In a traditional chronological format, here's what your resume might look like:

JOB HISTORY

1972 - 1985	Secretary
1970 - 1972	Bookkeeper
1968 - 1970	Office Clerk

Admit it: It doesn't look very good. Your last job ended in 1985. Your resume immediately reveals you were unemployed for more than a decade!

The solution

Take the focus off the dates, add special points to your Summary of Qualifications, and update your resume with new computer or technical skills.

Take the focus off the dates. Use a Functional Style Job History, Method 1, to de-emphasize job dates and focus on your experience and strengths instead.

Just list your job positions and titles without their dates, and that previous example gets turned into this functional style:

WORK EXPERIENCE

AS A SECRETARY:

AS A BOOKKEEPER:

AS AN OFFICE CLERK:

It's fixed. It's that simple. Your biggest worry has been taken care of. There are no dates here for an employer to judge you by, only your solid and relevant work experience.

Add special points to your Summary of Qualifications. Add a line or phrase to your Summary of Qualifications emphasizing your desire to get back into the workforce. For example, you could say "Eager to rebuild career" or "Very committed to reestablishing myself as a professional secretary."

In addition, if you've been getting ready for the new job market by learning computer programs or upgrading your skills, make sure to point this out, early on, in your Summary of Qualifications so that an employer can immediately feel secure that your skills are up to date, or at least becoming so.

Update yourself and your resume—take a computer course. If you're not technically up to date, it's time to do something about it. Sure, you can always list your old skills from that last job you held, but face it: If you're heading off the list with electric typewriters and keypunch machines, it won't be very impressive. Yes, you can always rename your Technical Skills section "Special Skills," and focus on other strong skills and features you possess instead, but that's only a temporary solution that probably won't get you very far. Accept that computers and technical skills are now essential for any type of office job. If you want to successfully find work, you'll have to make the latest technology a part of your life sooner or later. Why not sooner? Take that computer course now, proudly display your new skills on your resume, and be right up there with everyone else.

For a before and after sample resume of an Individual reentering the workforce, see pages 161 to 162.

Overqualifieds—How to Look Just Right for the Job You Want Now

You would think the more qualified you are, the better. Well, that's usually the case, but not always. You can be overqualified or too qualified if you're applying for a position that is several steps down from your current job level or from the jobs you've previously held. For whatever reason, whether you just want a change of pace or can't find the same level of employment as before, you're applying for something different, and that makes an employer wonder about you.

Think of it from an employer's point of view. Let's suppose *you* were doing the hiring. You're looking for a receptionist and among your stack of resumes appears one from an office manager. Immediately, questions arise, red flags go up. You would certainly wonder why an office manager is applying for this lower-level position. You might quickly attribute it to today's difficult job market, but the following concerns may very well still linger: You'll wonder if the applicant will be satisfied with lower pay than he or she is used to; or if he or she will be bored or unchallenged by the position and then not last very long; or even if this person knows enough to be a threat to your own job.

So, back in your own shoes now, if you think you might be overqualified for the type of job you're looking for, there are valid reasons why you need to cleverly present yourself in your resume. You must try to avoid looking too qualified and at the same time still give yourself credit for all the good and important work you've done. It requires a delicate balance but, trust me, you can do it.

The problem

Here's what your resume might look like in a traditional chronological format:

JOB OBJECTIVE: Receptionist

JOB HISTORY:

1993-1996 **EXECUTIVE SECRETARY**

1989-1993 **ADMINISTRATIVE ASSISTANT**

Here, your previous job positions simply make you look too qualified for the job you're currently after.

The solution

Use a Functional Style Job History, Method 2, to create a work experience section that is better geared to your current job goal.

Emphasize duties that relate best to the type of job you want now, group them into categories, give them new functional headings, and place the most important ones at the beginning of your Experience section, as in the following example:

JOB OBJECTIVE: Receptionist

WORK EXPERIENCE:

RECEPTION / PUBLIC CONTACT:

ADMINISTRATIVE EXPERIENCE:

Now you don't look overqualified anymore. In fact, you look just right. Your new functional headings help you focus on what's most important to the job you're applying for and make you look like an appropriate candidate.

Notice, however, that you don't completely ignore or eliminate your higher-level experience or abilities either. "Administrative Experience" still gets mentioned but only *after* you've sold your more important "Reception/Public Contact" experience first.

Irrelevant Job Positions—When You Have Too Many or They're in the Wrong Place

Suppose that you're a secretary or office worker but, along the way, you've sidetracked into different types of jobs. When it's time to put them all on your resume, you find you have more irrelevant jobs than relevant ones and they're dominating your resume. Or perhaps those irrelevant jobs just happen to be your most recent ones, and they're sticking out right at the top of your resume when they shouldn't be.

The problem

Your irrelevant positions are ruining the focus of your current job objective and making you look like you're not the best match for the job. In a chronological format, here's what your resume might look like:

JOB OBJECTIVE: A Secretarial position

JOB HISTORY:

1991-1996	**SALESPERSON**
1988-1991	**TEACHER**
1985-1988	**SECRETARY**
1983-1985	**REAL ESTATE AGENT**
1977-1983	**CLERK TYPIST**

Starting off your resume with irrelevant jobs just isn't effective, and your past secretarial jobs can't do much for you when they're sandwiched between irrelevant jobs.

The solution

Use a Functional Style Job History, Method 1, to freely position all relevant jobs at the beginning of your resume. Then you can play down or entirely omit the irrelevant ones and you'll end up with a much sharper, more focused Experience section, as in the following example:

JOB OBJECTIVE: A Secretarial position

RELEVANT EXPERIENCE:

AS A SECRETARY:

AS A CLERK TYPIST:

There, that's better. Problem solved. (For a sample before and after resume, see pages 149 to 151.)

Employment Gaps—How to Stop Them from Sticking Out

So there were periods of time when you were unemployed. We're all human, after all. But how do you handle those nasty employment gaps on your resume?

The problem

Your resume reveals employment gaps that make an employer wonder why you weren't working during that time.

In a traditional chronological format, your resume might look like the following:

JOB HISTORY:

| 1994 - 1996 | **GENERAL OFFICE CLERK** |
| 1990 - 1991 | **ACCOUNTING CLERK** |

There are no job positions listed for the time period from 1991 to 1994. Three years of unemployment are immediately revealed.

The solution

Use a Functional Style Job History, Method 1, to omit your job dates and focus on your job positions and experience instead. For instance, here's the above example turned into Functional Style:

WORK EXPERIENCE:

AS A GENERAL OFFICE CLERK:

AS AN ACCOUNTING CLERK:

No dates are visible now, so the problem is easily solved.

If you'd rather stay in the chronological format, there is a way to camouflage your dates, though possibly not as effectively. That is to place the dates on the right-hand side of the page rather than on the left, as in the following example:

JOB HISTORY:

| **GENERAL OFFICE CLERK:** | 1994-1996 |
| **ACCOUNTING CLERK:** | 1990-1991 |

Although it's a minor change, the eye still makes contact with your job positions and experiences first. (For a sample resume, see page 120.)

Short-Term Job Positions—How to Avoid Looking Like a Job Hopper

You consider yourself lucky. You've pretty much always kept yourself employed. You've held all types of office jobs—some long, some short, whatever the length of time, as long as you kept working, everything's fine, right? Well, you might feel fine until you put it all together on your resume and find yourself with a string of short-term jobs. Your job dates might look like the following:

1995-1996

1994-1995

1993-1994

1992-1993

The problem

A listing of short-term jobs on your resume gives the appearance that you haven't been able to hold a steady job, and it can make an employer wonder about your stability as an employee.

The solution

First of all, as you are painfully aware, today's employment situation is different from that of the past. Because of the difficult job market—cutbacks, downsizing, layoffs, etc.—employees have been forced out of what might otherwise have been long-term positions. This new job climate has required that job hunters take whatever they can get—temp work, agency work, or short-term assignments. Many employers appreciate the difficulties and recognize this trend. However, there are things you can do to your resume to help it along.

Specify the reason—if it's a good one. If you have a good reason for your short-term jobs, be sure to let an employer know it. For instance, if your short-term jobs were temporary placements or short-term assignments, then say so. Mention it under the job dates, as in the following example:

| 1995-1996 | **RECEPTIONIST** |
| (temporary placement) | |

In this case, all doubts are immediately cleared with an explanation for this short-term position.

If you've held many temporary placement jobs, you can set them off with an explanatory heading, as in the following example:

Various temporary assignments through Hunter Personnel:

| 1995-1996 | **DICTA TYPIST** |
| 1994 | **CLERK** |

Streamline your dates. If you held jobs for less than a year in length, you can leave them off entirely, as long as they don't create any noticeable gaps and they're not important to the job you're applying for now. However, if they are important to the job you're applying for now and you must keep them on your resume, instead of reporting them like this:

November 1994-January 1995

try this—leave out the months, so it reads:

1994-1995

Presto! You've lengthened your job time. Don't worry, you're allowed to do it. Employers are perfectly used to seeing years only, without the months, in today's streamlined resumes.

Eliminate or summarize nonessential short-term jobs. If your short-term jobs are not important to the job you're applying for now because they're old or less relevant, you can either eliminate them entirely or, if you wish, combine them into one summarizing sentence. You can go from what might have looked like this:

1991-1992	PAYROLL CLERK
1990-1991	DATA ENTRY CLERK
1989-1990	FILE CLERK
1988-1989	CLERK

to this:

1988-1992   Held clerical positions in various organizations throughout
              New York.

By turning your nonessential jobs into summarizing background information, you fix your short-term job date problem while still getting to show an employer the extent of your working experience. (For a sample before and after resume, see pages 129 to 131.)

Try the Functional Style format. Of course, you can always use the Functional Style format, if you wish. Again, this puts all dates out of the picture for a while (at least long enough to pique an employer's interest in you).

In Conclusion

You've done everything it takes to make your resume the best one for you. You might have adopted a Functional Style Resume or kept it in the chronological format, just adding a few tricks to help it along.

It's time now to go on to the sample resumes where you will view all kinds of before and after resumes in both the chronological and functional formats. So get ready to see resumes transformed before your very eyes in "From Mediocre to Magnificent," up next.

8

From Mediocre to Magnificent

Sixteen Sample Resumes Transformed

Until now, you've learned how to create your resume part by part, section by section, piece by piece. Now it's time to see how everything works together as a whole.

The sample resumes in this chapter are probably your most important resume-writing tools of all. There's nothing like learning from the real thing: real-life sample resumes complete with before and after versions and commentaries on their dramatic transformations.

So before preparing your resume's final draft, carefully analyze the ones in this chapter. You will see that even the most mundane resumes can be turned into powerful winners—resumes that get noticed and that can help you learn to make yours stand out from the pack!

In this chapter you will:

- See how all the resume parts come together to form a fabulous, enticing resume.
- See how a professional layout and appearance can create a powerful new impression.
- Identify with resume scenarios similar to your own, and gain valuable ideas and inspiration for the layout and content of your own.
- Learn to avoid common resume blunders by viewing the mistakes of others.
- Pick up tips and tricks to make yourself look good even when you're not perfect.

- Witness how the tailoring aspect, like a pulsating vein, runs through the whole resume to give it the life and extra edge it needs.
- Learn to modify your resume to fit different job positions.

So sit back and travel what are almost the final miles of your resume-writing journey.

Presenting ... the Before and Afters

The following are real-life resumes. Only names and addresses have been changed.

1. Secretary/Receptionist
2. Medical Secretary
3. Legal Secretary
4. Legal Secretary
5. Executive Secretary/Administrative Assistant
6. Administrative Assistant
7. Accounts Receivable Clerk
   Secretary/Office Clerk
8. Customer Service Clerk
   Accounting Clerk
9. Customer Service Representative
10. Data Entry Operator
11. Data Processor
12. Bookkeeper
13. Medical Secretary—New Grad
14. Receptionist—Career Changer
15. Financial Clerk—Reentering the Workforce
16. Office Clerk—Overqualified
    Office Manager

How to get the most out of the sample resumes

Analyze each sample before resume and the commentary box for background information on each candidate. Review the side comments for specific information on how to fix each resume. Then read the after version and compare. You be the judge of the effect from "Before" to "After."

Rhonda Rice
11 Salinger Court
Dallas, Texas 10002
(123) 555-8635

Rhonda is a multitalented secretary with fantastic computer abilities, but you'd never know it from her "Before" resume. She fails to elaborate on her secretarial experience, lists unrelated sales and cashier jobs, and places irrelevant fashion courses smack at the top!

| Needs a Job Objective and Summary of Qualifications. |

EDUCATION

September 1987 - June 1992

LAMBERT TECHNICAL SCHOOL
Dallas, Texas
* Secondary School Diploma
* Fashion Arts Program (Major)
* Fashion Arts Diploma

| Position Education after Experience. |

WORK EXPERIENCE

October 1994 - Present

WINE SHOPS OF AMERICA
46 Duncan Street, 2nd Floor, Head office

* <u>DEPARTMENTAL SECRETARY</u>

Reported to the Director of Specialty Services and Director of Traffic, Customs and Excise.

<u>Duties included:</u>
Generating reports, compiling data, word processing, filing, reception and distributing mail.

| Provide detailed secretarial duties. |

May 1994 - June 1994

TONY'S MEN'S SHOP
Hwy 6 & Banton Blvd. (Westin Center)

* <u>PART-TIME HEAD CASHIER</u>

<u>Duties included:</u>
Preparing and completing Daily Summary Reports, training new cashiers and operating cash registers.

October 1992 - December 1993

BRIGHTON COMPANY
725 Long Street (Long & Milton Ave.)

* <u>SALES REPRESENTATIVE</u>

<u>Duties included:</u>
Customer sales and service, merchandising and operating cash registers.

| Omit irrelevant jobs. |

* <u>TEMPORARY OFFICE CLERK</u>
<u>Duties included:</u>
Filing and typing.

COMPUTER SKILLS

Experienced in WP 6.0 for Windows, MS Word, WP 5.1, Avery Label Pro and Flow 3

| Provide full list of skills. |

REFERENCES

Available upon request.

Rhonda comes alive in her "After" resume. A tailored Summary of Qualifications, enhanced Work Experience section, and complete rundown of technical skills prove what a highly capable secretary she is (and ultimately resulted in getting her the job!).

RHONDA RICE
11 Salinger Court
Dallas, Texas 10002
(123) 555-8635

OBJECTIVE

To work as a secretary/receptionist.

SUMMARY OF QUALIFICATIONS

Experienced secretary with proven ability to handle a wide range of office tasks. Excellent computer knowledge including WordPerfect for Windows 6.0. Exceptionally fast learner - can easily master any new computer program. Pleasant professional telephone manner. Fast worker, very neat and organized.

WORK EXPERIENCE

1994 - Present   **DEPARTMENTAL SECRETARY**
Wine Shops of America - Head Office, Dallas TX

Provided administrative and secretarial support to two directors and performed secretarial duties for a Distribution Department of eight managers.

* Typed letters, internal memos, lists, reports and general correspondence using computers and typewriters.
* Designed, proofread and edited various computer-generated forms.
* Created banners and flyers for special events using computer graphics.
* Processed daily spreadsheets. Greeted visitors arriving for meetings.
* Answered large volume of incoming calls; took messages, transferred calls, dealt with general inquiries and redirected callers to correct departments.
* Scheduled and coordinated all appointments, interdepartmental meetings and conferences.
* Recorded attendance and completed weekly time cards for directors and five managers.
* Ordered supplies, equipment and office stationery.
* Maintained office equipment. Helped troubleshoot machines needing repair. Instructed managers and staff on use of equipment.
* Completed travel expense sheets and assisted with travel arrangements for vice president, directors and managers.
* Reentered and updated annual budget revisions on computer.
* Opened, sorted and distributed large amounts of daily incoming mail.

Special Achievements:

* Taught vice president's administrative assistant how to use newly installed flow chart software program.
* Took initiative to routinely help clear typing, filing and mail backlog of vice president's secretary.

EDUCATION

1993   **COMPUTER TRAINING COURSE - WORDPERFECT 5.1**
            Computer World Services, Dallas

1987-1992   **SECONDARY SCHOOL DIPLOMA**
            Lambert Technical School, Dallas

TECHNICAL SKILLS AND SPECIAL ABILITIES

Possess wide range of computer skills:
* Excellent knowledge of Windows, WordPerfect 6.0 and 5.1, Microsoft Word 6.0, Lotus 1-2-3, Avery Label Pro, and Flow 3
* Familiar with Harvard Graphics
* Presently learning Excel
* Thoroughly up to date with latest computer software
* Can teach self to operate any computer program

Familiar with the following office equipment:
* IBM computers, IBM and Hewlett-Packard laser printers, fax machines, photocopiers, calculators, voice mail and VCRs for conferences.

Other abilities include:
* Graphics and spreadsheets
* Excellent English skills
* Accurate keyboarding abilities
* Proofreading and editing
* Bright, creative and eager to learn

REFERENCES

Attached. Further references available upon request.

Sandra Inglis
42 Willowcreek Road
Teaneck, New Jersey 10002
(123) 555-7371

Needs a Job Objective and Summary of Qualifications.

Sandra's "Before" resume is in desperate need of an overhaul. There are no visible job or course titles, and her job duties are extremely weak and scanty. Though Sandra lacks computer skills, she has good, solid working experience. She sells herself short, however, with this poorly formed resume.

Education

1979-1982

Dellview High School, Graduation Diploma

Feb 1990-May 1990

Position Education after Job History.

Miller's Business College Medical Secretary

Employment History

June-July 1990

Dr. Reginald Locke, Dr. Colin Wong, M.D.
Cedar Valley Medical Dental Center

Duties, Responsibilities   Omit space-wasting headings.

Book appointments by phone
Take out medical records for patients
Medical billing, order medication when required.

Sept 1990-August 1993

Dr. J. B. Lamont, M.D.
8680 King Street, Sherwood Medical Clinic

Duties, Responsibilities

Answering phone, booking appointments, booking appointments for specialists such as abdominal ultrasounds, gallbladders, pelvic, obstetrical, etc.
Emergency blue sheets
Typing reports for lawyers   Turn weak duties into powerful job descriptions.
Filing medical submission cards
Pharmacy prescriptions orders

Hobbies and Interests

Cooking, exercising, sewing   Omit hobbies.

Languages

English (fluent), Italian (speak)

References

        Kate Armstrong, Public Health Nurse
        25 Amex Avenue, Teaneck, NJ | Print references on separate sheet. |
        (123) 555-3669

        James Norris, Teacher
        270 Field Avenue, Teaneck, NJ
        (123) 555-1900

        Lauretta Escott, Medical Secretary
        34 Millpond Road, Fairlawn, NJ
        (123) 555-6472

Career Aims, Goals | Omit awkward career goal. |

        I wish to work in an achievement-oriented atmosphere where I can receive the kind of training necessary to make me a more valuable person.

SANDRA INGLIS
42 Willowcreek Road, Teaneck, New Jersey 10002   *(123) 555-7371*

JOB OBJECTIVE:

Sandra's new, professionalized resume effectively sells her best strengths, job experience, and skills.

A medical secretarial position.

SUMMARY OF QUALIFICATIONS:

Highly dependable. Three years' medical secretarial experience. Excellent people skills. Accurate typing abilities. Hardworking and self-motivated.

EMPLOYMENT HISTORY:

1990-1993   **MEDICAL SECRETARY**
             Dr. J. B. Lamont, General Practitioner
             Sherwood Medical Clinic, Fairlawn, NJ

- Booked a multitude of inter-office patient appointments and hospital procedures including minor surgeries, specialists' appointments, blood work, physicals, CAT scans, ultrasounds and x-rays.
- Answered phones which included handling patient inquiries and concerns, relaying messages and transferring calls.
- Handled busy patient flow including registering incoming patients and preparing their medical files.
- Instructed patients, in a clear and reassuring manner, on how to prepare for tests and procedures.
- Interpreted and clarified doctor's instructions to non-English-speaking patients.
- Recorded billings and consistently updated and maintained patient health insurance information.
- Typed medicolegal reports and referral letters.
- Completed lab and x-ray requisitions, hospital emergency forms, sick leave forms and WCB papers.
- Filed patient charts, hospital reports and insurance forms using alphabetical filing systems.

1990   **MEDICAL SECRETARY**
             Dr. Reginald Locke, Dr. Colin Wong
             Cedar Valley Medical Dental Center, Passaic, NJ

- Principal duties and responsibilities similar in nature to those described above.

EDUCATION:

1990   **MEDICAL SECRETARIAL PROGRAM**
             Miller's Business College, Teaneck

1979-1982   **GRADUATION DIPLOMA**
             Dellview High School, Teaneck

SPECIAL SKILLS AND ABILITIES:

Solid knowledge of medical terminology. Speak Italian fluently. Electronic memory telephones. Photocopier. Answering machines. Eager to learn. Very organized and efficient.

REFERENCES AVAILABLE UPON REQUEST

CATHERINE WELLS
89 Canyon Road
Chicago, IL 10002
(123) 555-5375

Catherine's "Before" resume starts off with a clear Job Objective and not a bad Skills section, but she incorrectly positions her Education first, heads off her Work Experience with an irrelevant piano teaching job, and tucks away her most important legal secretarial positions on a second page.

JOB OBJECTIVE: **AN ENTRY LEVEL POSITION AS A LEGAL SECRETARY**

SKILLS:
- Familiar with legal office procedures and terminology
- Proficient in WordPerfect 5.2/6.0 for Windows
- Proficient in WordPerfect 5.1
- Keyboarding speed 60 wpm (English)
- Keyboarding speed 30 wpm (Russian)
- Knowledgeable in typing correspondence
- Fluent in English and Russian

EDUCATION:
1992-1994

STANTON COLLEGE OF APPLIED ARTS AND TECHNOLOGY
Chicago, Illinois

> Position Education after Experience.

OFFICE ADMINISTRATION - LEGAL DIPLOMA PROGRAM
Studies included Machine Transcription, Advanced Information Processing, and Accounting
Honors Graduate

1991-1992

WESTLAND HEIGHTS SECONDARY SCHOOL
Chicago, Illinois
Honors Graduate

1985-1988

VIRSK COLLEGE
Russia

> Omit irrelevant course.

MUSIC DIPLOMA PROGRAM
Studies included Conducting, Methodology of Musical Education in School, and Psychology

BUSINESS EXPERIENCE:
1993-Present

Piano Teacher

> Omit irrelevant jobs.

- Teaching pre-schoolers to love and understand music
- Specializing in piano lessons
- Giving a background in music history
- Preparing for recitals

1994-1995 **Johnson, MacDougal and Associates**
Chicago, Illinois

RECEPTIONIST and LEGAL SECRETARY

- Switchboard relief
- Transcribed correspondence
- Prepared court documents

Provide detailed job duties.

1994   **Elliot Hopkins, Esq.**
Chicago, Illinois

LEGAL SECRETARY

- Switchboard relief
- Scheduled appointments
- Prepared court documents and correspondence
- Assisted clients in translations from Russian to English and from English to Russian

1992   **Mike's Complete Car Care Services Limited**
Chicago, Illinois

RECEPTIONIST
- Scheduled appointments
- Filing
- Handled cash

1993 (summer) **Cityscape Real Estate Services Limited**
Chicago, Illinois

RECEPTIONIST

- Typed correspondence, using WP 5.1
- Answered telephone
- Filing
- Scheduled appointments

Omit interests.

INTERESTS: Computers, traveling, music (piano), cooking

REFERENCES: Available upon request

119

CATHERINE WELLS
89 Canyon Road, Chicago, IL 10002   (123) 555-5375

JOB OBJECTIVE:

Legal Secretarial Position

SUMMARY OF QUALIFICATIONS:

- Experienced legal secretary with excellent word processing skills.
- Familiar with several computer programs including WordPerfect-Windows 6.0.
- Excellent organizational abilities and oral communication skills.
- Loyal, detail-oriented and willing to learn.

Here, all irrelevant jobs and courses were eliminated to make Catherine's new resume live and breathe "legal secretary" on one sleek page.

WORK EXPERIENCE:

LEGAL SECRETARY/RECEPTIONIST

Johnson, MacDougal and Associates, Chicago 1994-1995

- Prepared court documents, financial statements and letters.
- Answered calls, handled inquiries, and greeted clients.
- Transcribed correspondence from machine and oral dictation.

LEGAL SECRETARY

Elliot Hopkins, Esq., Chicago 1994

Provided secretarial support and performed reception duties for two lawyers specializing in family and criminal law.

- Prepared court documents - notice of motions and judgments.
- Drafted and typed correspondence to clients and Legal Aid.
- Transcribed large amounts of legal dicta tapes.
- Completed applications for Immigration and Refugee Board.
- Monitored and recorded client billings on computer.
- Acted as interpreter for lawyers and clients; interviewed Russian clients, and obtained accurate information for the completion of immigration forms.
- Answered calls from lawyers, clients, courts, and technical support staff; handled inquiries and provided information.
- Scheduled all appointments and meetings.
- Coordinated travel and business arrangements.
- Opened new client files and maintained alpha-numerical filing system.
- Deposited money, wrote checks, issued receipts, and handled petty cash.
- Maintained office equipment, arranged for repair when necessary.
- Opened, sorted and distributed mail for entire office.

EDUCATION:

OFFICE ADMINISTRATION - LEGAL DIPLOMA PROGRAM

Stanton College of Applied Arts and Technology, Chicago   1992-1994
Honors Graduate

TECHNICAL SKILLS AND SPECIAL ABILITIES:

WordPerfect 6.0 (Windows), 5.2 and 5.1. Keyboarding 60 w.p.m. Russian keyboarding 30 w.p.m. Machine transcription skills. Fax, copiers, laser printers. Good command of legal terminology. Familiar with immigration, criminal and labor law. Fluent in Russian.

REFERENCES AVAILABLE UPON REQUEST

Emily Channer
6533 King Street
Apt. 507
Minneapolis, MN 10002
(123) 555-0199

> Emily's "Before" resume simply contains too much. She lists too many jobs in crowded, wordy paragraphs that make her resume a chore to read.

> Needs a Job Objective.

SUMMARY OF QUALIFICATIONS

- Seven years of legal secretary experience, experience in business, corporate finance, family, litigation, tax and trademarks
- Over four years of executive secretary experience in trading and food manufacturing
- Two years of secretary experience in factory
- Function well in fast-paced, high-pressure atmosphere
- Adapt easily to new concepts and responsibilities
- Adept at working independently and as a team member, good interpersonal skill in dealing with a diversity of professionals, clients, and staff members

> Scale down Summary.

KNOWLEDGE OF COMPUTER APPLICATIONS

Microsoft Word, WordPerfect 5.1, Chinese Microsoft Word, WANG, Mass-11 and computer modem

WORKING EXPERIENCE

Dec 95 - Present

J. Thomas Reardon, Esq. Minneapolis
Legal Secretary
Part-time experience in litigation and family law. General legal secretarial duties.

Jul 93 - Jun 95

Beatty and Hopkins - Hong Kong
Legal Secretary
Experience in business, corporate finance and family. Principal duties and responsibilities were similar in nature to those discussed below in Emerson & McDonald. However, since this was the only swing-shift position, I was involved in and solely responsible for all activities pertaining to secretarial functions, including general office duties.

Jan 89 - Jul 93

Emerson and MacDonald - Hong Kong

> Streamline job descriptions and layout.

Legal Secretary
Experience in commercial, tax, litigation and trademarks. Typing and proofreading documents (English and Chinese); photocopying, assembling and distributing prepared materials, taking shorthand notes, transcribing letters and memos, screening telephone calls, scheduling for meetings, closings, communicating with clients and other counsel, ensuring that deadlines were met, taking care of the statements for billing to clients, completing complex clerical procedures in connection therewith, organizing and maintaining accounting records and petty cash accounts for submission to the accounting department; sending messages by telex and facsimile machines.

Mar 87 - Dec 88

> Manor Industries (International) Ltd.
>
> Eliminate or summarize older, nonlegal positions.
>
> *Secretary to Finance & Administration Manager*
> Transcribing and typing minutes of conferences and meetings, memos, reports, statements and so on from written notes or verbal instructions; maintaining confidential filing systems; responsible for maintaining a calendar of appointments and meetings; screening telephone calls and visitors; handling senior executives' personnel, medical, insurance and salary; monitoring telex and facsimile machines for incoming messages.

Aug 83 - Mar 87

> Mesotronic Limited
> *Secretary to Managing Director*
> General running of the office, ordering, issuing, and controlling inventory on all office supplies and business equipment; receiving and perusing all incoming mail, as well as redirecting it to appropriate staff members for action; ensuring that all filing systems were properly maintained; preparing and processing imports/exports and banking documents for signature; typing and composing of letters and memos; and bookkeeping.

Jun 80 - Aug 82

> Chang Aluminum Co.
> *Secretary to the Proprietor*
> Principal duties and responsiblities were similar in nature to those mentioned in Mesotronic Limited.

EDUCATION

Sep 87 - Jun 88

> The Technical School of Hong Kong
> Company Secretarial Course
> Passed ICSA Part I - Economics, GP Law and Part II - Accounting

Sep 84 - Jun 86

> Harrison Technical School
> Certificate: Company Secretaryship
> Passed LLC Higher English, Economics, Intermediate Bookkeeping

Sep 82 - Aug 83

> Mary Foster College
> Diploma: Executive Secretarial Studies

Sep 80 - Jun 82
St. Vincent College
Passed GCE "O" - Math, Econonomics, Biology

Jun 80 - Aug 80
Hong Kong Women's Association
Certificate: Summer Business Secretarial Studies

Sep 77 - Jun 80
Wordsworth College
Passed HKCEE - 8 Subjects passed including English Language and English History

EMILY CHANNER
6533 King Street, #507
Minneapolis, MN 10002
(123) 555-0199

Emily's "After" resume is more inviting. Notice that we focused on her legal secretarial positions and summed up her less relevant executive secretarial jobs in one quick sentence.

LEGAL SECRETARY

SUMMARY OF QUALIFICATIONS

- Seven years' legal secretarial experience.
- Familiar with business, commercial, corporate finance, family, criminal, litigation, tax and trademarks law.
- Fast accurate keyboarding and excellent dicta-typing skills.
- Function well in fast-paced, high-pressure environment.
- Work well independently or as part of a team.

EMPLOYMENT EXPERIENCE

1995-Present   <u>**LEGAL SECRETARY**</u>
J. Thomas Reardon, Esq., Minneapolis

- Typed various legal documents such as litigation forms, notice of motions and affidavits.
- Opened new client files and maintained filing system.

1993-1995   <u>**LEGAL SECRETARY**</u>
Beatty and Hopkins, Hong Kong

- Transcribed and proofread urgent corporate documents, letters and memos for seven lawyers.
- Worked efficiently requiring little or no supervision.

1989-1993   <u>**LEGAL SECRETARY**</u>
Emerson and MacDonald, Hong Kong

Held positions in the Taxation, Commercial and Trademarks departments of this large firm with over 100 lawyers.
- Managed heavy dicta-typing load - transcribed and proofread English and Chinese documents including contracts 10 to 30 pages in length.
- Answered phones - screened calls, recorded and relayed messages.
- Scheduled all client appointments and meetings.
- Booked and coordinated travel arrangements for conferences.
- Ensured that all deadlines were met for joint venture contracts.
- Handled all billing statements - calculated fees and invoiced clients.
- Organized and maintained accounting records and petty cash accounts.
- Updated and maintained files.

1980-1988   Held executive secretarial positions at various Hong Kong manufacturing companies.

EDUCATION AND TRAINING

1987-1988	COMPANY SECRETARIAL COURSE, The Technical School of Hong Kong
1984-1986	COMPANY SECRETARYSHIP, Harrison Technical School, Hong Kong
1982-1983	EXECUTIVE SECRETARIAL STUDIES, Mary Foster College, Hong Kong
1980-1982	MATH/ECONOMICS, St. Vincent College, Hong Kong
1980	BUSINESS SECRETARIAL STUDIES, Hong Kong Women's Association
1977-1980	ENGLISH/HISTORY, Wordsworth College, Hong Kong

TECHNICAL SKILLS AND SPECIAL ABILITIES

- Microsoft Word, WordPerfect 5.1, Mass 11, Chinese Microsoft Word and Twi-Bridge.
- Wang computers, modems, telex, facsimile.
- Machine transcription, keyboarding 75 wpm, shorthand 100 wpm, minute taking, bookkeeping.
- Serious worker with good interpersonal skills.

LANGUAGES

Mandarin, Cantonese and some Japanese.

REFERENCES AVAILABLE UPON REQUEST

CONNIE McKAY   Res. 123-555-3412
900 Main Street
New York, NY 10002

Connie is an executive secretary with impressive working experience. Her job titles are not easily noticeable, but she does provide nice job detail. Her resume is generally a good one which just needs some polishing up.

Needs a Job Objective.

SKILLS:
Administrative	Typing	Leadership
Organizational	Dictaphone	Interpersonal
Shorthand	WordPerfect for Windows 6.0	

EXPERIENCE:

1986 -1995   LANDEX INC., NEW YORK, NY

Bold job titles.

Assistant to the Senior Vice President, Corporate Finance & Treasurer

Responsibilities: Omit space-wasting headings.

Add a Main Function.

- Ability to take charge of multi-confidential tasks efficiently and productively
- Coordinate meetings with various government/banking/university/real estate committees
- Maintain control on letters of credit and act as a liaison between banks and project coordinators.
- Prepare annual departmental budget and maintain control over forecast.
- Process invoices, check requisitions and expense reports
- Coordinate activities for various fundraising campaigns
- Coordinate travel arrangements and maintain numerous mailing lists
- Personal assistance (banking, appointments, etc.)

1976-1986   TENOX, HEAD OFFICE, NEW YORK

1985-1986   Executive Secretary to the Assistant to the President and Chief Executive Officer

Responsibilities:

- Participated on various corporate committees
- Diverse secretarial duties

1976-1985   Analyst, Office Systems

Responsibilities:

- Installed software and provided maintenance for IBM 8100 word processing system at Tenox's nine locations in the U.S.
- Provided ongoing training and support to 160 WP users
- Designed and implemented WP Training and Electronic Mail courses exclusively for Tenox.
- Acted as liaison between IBM and Tenox Office Systems Group

Connie McKay
Page 2

EDUCATION   High School - Honors Diploma
                   Business/Secretarial Certificate

| List courses as skills. | Various courses in Public Speaking, Presentation Seminars, Leadership Skills, Time
                   Management, Computer Technology, French

HOBBIES   Sailing, Gardening, Jazz, Reading, Traveling | Omit hobbies. |

REFERENCES AVAILABLE UPON REQUEST

Now, Connie's job titles stand out at a glance. Also, her job dates were purposely highlighted to show off her steady continuous employment. And by adding the magnitude of the companies she worked for, we made this resume stronger than ever.

CONNIE McKAY

900 Main Street, New York, NY 10002

(123) 555-3412

ADMINISTRATIVE ASSISTANT / EXECUTIVE SECRETARY

SUMMARY:

Extensive administrative experience. Excellent organizational and interpersonal skills. Computer literate. Good at meeting deadlines and handling pressure situations. Very reliable and flexible.

EXPERIENCE:

1986-1995   **ADMINISTRATIVE ASSISTANT**
Landex Inc., New York, NY

Provided administrative and secretarial support to the Senior Vice President, Corporate Finance Group, of this large North American real estate development company with 4,000 employees.

- Took charge of multi-confidential tasks efficiently and productively.
- Coordinated meetings with various government, banking, university and real estate committees.
- Maintained control on hundreds of letters of credit, and acted as liaison between banks and project coordinators.
- Prepared annual departmental budget and maintained control over forecast.
- Processed invoices, check requisitions and expense reports.
- Organized activities for various fundraising campaigns.
- Coordinated travel arrangements and maintained numerous mailing lists.
- Provided personal assistance - banking, appointments, etc.

1985-1986   **EXECUTIVE SECRETARY**
Tenox, Head Office, New York, NY

Provided administrative and secretarial support to Assistant to the President and CEO of this major international oil company with 6,000 employees.

- Participated on various corporate committees including safety, social and arts committees; attended meetings, produced brochures, etc.
- Performed diverse secretarial duties including typing and accounting.

1976-1985   **SYSTEMS ANALYST**
Tenox, Head Office, New York, NY

- Installed software and provided maintenance for IBM 8100 Word Processing System at Tenox's nine locations across the U.S.
- Provided ongoing training and support to 160 WP users.
- Designed and implemented WP training and electronic mail courses exclusively for Tenox.
- Acted as liaison between IBM and Tenox Office Systems Group.

EDUCATION:

Business/Secretarial Certificate, St. Elizabeth's College, Albany
Various career-related workshops and seminars, Landex, Tenox, New York

PROFESSIONAL SKILLS:

WordPerfect for Windows 6.0, keyboarding 80 wpm, Pitman shorthand 80 wpm, dictaphone, public speaking, leadership abilities, excellent time management skills, French, familiar with all types of office machines and equipment.

REFERENCES AVAILABLE UPON REQUEST

SUSAN LAWRENCE
10 Holbrook Street
St. Louis, Missouri 10002
(123) 555-2918

> Susan's "Before" resume starts off with a nice skills section, but she fills her important Administrative Assistant position with weak job duties and then lists a string of extremely short-term jobs which do more harm than good.

> Needs a Job Objective.

SPECIAL SKILLS

* working knowledge of Windows 95, Word 2.0, Lotus 1-2-3, and WordPerfect 6.0.
* excellent interpersonal skills
* ability to cooperate positively and enthusiastically in a team environment.
* highly motivated and eager to accept new challenges.
* efficient organizational skills.

EMPLOYMENT HISTORY

Feb. 1994 - Present   **National Bank,** *Secretary / Admin. Assistant*
St. Louis, Missouri

> Enhance Job Duties.

* opening new mortgages, loans, accounts, and investments on the banking system
* making mortgage/loan payments, modifications
* closing and paying in full mortgages/loans
* receive and organize mortgage / loan security documentation
* access and print credit bureaus
* typing, filing, answering telephone calls
* performing teller duties when needed

Dec. 1993   **City Bank, GM Visa Center,** *Intermediate Clerk*
St. Louis, Missouri

> Eliminate or summarize less relevant short-term jobs

* opening, sorting and distributing mail
* separating and filing daily reports
* answering telephone calls, faxing, photocopying
* inputting cancellations on the system

Nov. 9-21 1993   **Farmer's Country Fair 1993,** *School Tours*
Information & Tour Assistant, St. Louis

* organizing and keeping students under control using loudspeaker
* answering and solving teachers' questions and concerns
* preparing and sending out tour kits
* general office duties

Feb. - Aug. 1991	**Conroy Suites Hotel,** _Sales Assistant / Banquet staff_

* Sales duties included: using WordPerfect 5.0 to type letters, update corporate files
* making brochures for clients
* answering telephone calls, making files, filing, typing memos, photocopying and faxing
* Banquet duties included: Setting tables, preparing food, serving, and general clean-up duties

Jun. - Aug. 1990	**Jetson Insurance Company,** _Filer / Microfilmer_

* filing and pulling policies
* microfilming policies and claims

EDUCATION

Sept. 1992 - 1993	**Trenton College,** St. Louis, Missouri

* Graphic Sign Design & Production

Sept. 1989 - 1992	**Dale Swanson Collegiate Institute,** St. Louis

* Graduated Honors with Art and Law awards
* received S.S.G.D. Diploma

* References available upon request.

SUSAN LAWRENCE
10 Holbrook Street
St. Louis, MO 10002
(123) 555-2918

In Susan's "After" resume, we combined her less relevant short-term jobs into one summarizing line. We turned her weak Administrative Assistant duties into powerful job descriptions and added a Main Function to reveal the full scope of her job.

OBJECTIVE

Administrative Assistant

SUMMARY OF QUALIFICATIONS

* Experienced Administrative Assistant with excellent interpersonal and organizational skills.
* Working knowledge of various computer software programs.
* Highly motivated and eager to accept new challenges.
* Cooperative, polite and hardworking.

WORK EXPERIENCE

1994-Present   **ADMINISTRATIVE ASSISTANT**
                     National Bank, St. Louis

Promoted from Teller/Secretary to Administrative Assistant within four months. Provided administrative support to three managers, and performed secretarial duties for entire branch of 11 tellers.

- Input mortgages, loan payments and investments on the banking system.
- Accessed and printed credit bureaus on personal and commercial accounts.
- Processed GIC and RRSP contribution certificates on computer.
- Assembled and organized all loan security documents.
- Created form letters for loans, mortgages, accounts, and investments.
- Typed reports using WP 6.0.
- Scheduled all appointments and client meetings for managers.
- Recorded minutes for all staff meetings.
- Ordered supplies and stationery for entire branch, and monitored and paid all branch expense bills.
- Developed and maintained close personal rapport with customers and clients.
- Answered 50 incoming calls per day; provided clients with information on new RRSP products and rates.
- Stayed overtime to serve clients; took initiative to work weekends to help clear any backlogs.
- Praised by manager as an asset to the company who gets along well with customers and staff.

1990-1993   Held clerical positions at City Bank and various other St. Louis companies and organizations.

EDUCATION

1994   INTERPERSONAL COMMUNICATION SKILLS, Fireside College, St. Louis
1992-1993   GRAPHIC SIGN DESIGN & PRODUCTION, Trenton College, St. Louis
1989-1992   SSGD DIPLOMA (with Honors), Dale Swanson Collegiate, St. Louis

TECHNICAL SKILLS

Windows 95, WordPerfect 6.0 and 5.1, Word 2.0, Lotus 1-2-3. IBM Computers, Panasonic electronic typewriter, postage machine, encoders, protectograph, calculators.

REFERENCES AVAILABLE UPON REQUEST

Cheryl's "Before" resume lacks direction. She tries to encompass every different type of job she wants into one Objective. She needs to concentrate on one job at a time. For Cheryl, we formed two resume versions, each one geared to a specific job position.

CHERYL BENSON
44 Cedar Hill Street
San Francisco, CA 10002
(123) 555-0244

Focus on one position.

OBJECTIVE   A secretarial, data entry, receptionist or clerical position.

PROFILE
* 4 years' varied experience in data entry and clerical field.
* Dependable, hard working
* Team player who works well with others

EDUCATION

Position Education after Job History.

CAREERS FIRST BUSINESS COLLEGE
Office Skills 1994
WordPerfect 5.1, WordPerfect 6.0, Lotus 1-2-3, data entry, basic accounting, typing 35 w.p.m., Business/English communications

SOMERSET COLLEGE
Career Development Workshop, Employment Skills, 1992

EMPLOYMENT HISTORY

Esson Gas, San Francisco, CA   1993-1994
Assistant

Emphasize duties relevant to a specific Objective.

* Provided clerical services and office support to the manager
* Managed shipping/receiving
* Handled staff scheduling
* Performed weekly accounting procedures

Star Taxi, Sacramento, CA   1991-1992
Data Entry/Accounting Clerk

* Provided general clerical duties
* Performed accounting procedures for accounts receivable and accounts payable
* Prepared monthly billing statements and payroll
* Processed orders and computerized billing

Confederation Trust Company (of California) 1990-1991
Computer Operator

* Executed batch jobs
* Generated and distributed computer reports
* Performed backups on AS/400 computer
* Analyzed program errors

REFERENCES AVAILABLE UPON REQUEST

For Cheryl's first "After" resume, we used the Functional Style format to group together and emphasize duties most relevant to her Accounts Receivable Job Objective. At the same time, her string of short-term job dates were deemphasized at the bottom of her resume.

CHERYL BENSON
44 Cedar Hill Street, San Francisco, CA 10002   *(123) 555-0244*

Accounts Receivable Clerk

QUALIFICATIONS

Experienced Accounting Clerk with excellent knowledge of accounts receivable and good data entry skills. Operate several computer programs including Lotus 1-2-3. Work well under pressure. Good public relations skills. Quick learner, dependable and hardworking.

RELEVANT EXPERIENCE

ACCOUNTING/DATA ENTRY:

- Performed weekly accounting procedures for accounts receivable/payable using computerized systems.
- Prepared, verified and issued monthly billing statements, and balanced monthly cash flow transactions.
- As Accounting Clerk with Star Taxi - processed route orders of hundreds of drivers and consistently verified their accuracy with dispatchers.
- As Assistant for Esson - calculated totals of all car wash vouchers and coupons for accountant.

PUBLIC RELATIONS:

- As Accounting Clerk with Star Taxi - regularly handled complaints and satisfied customers by locating source of monthly statement errors and bringing them to manager's attention.
- Consistently tended to all customer problems and needs. Was very helpful to drivers, staff and coworkers.

OFFICE SUPPORT:

- Filed and maintained statements, company and customer records.
- Answered and redirected incoming calls and recorded messages.
- Handled inquiries regarding accounts.
- Typed and edited letters and memos using a word processor.
- Handled temporary and permanent staff scheduling.
- Purchased goods and supplies. Effectively prioritized tasks.

TECHNICAL SKILLS AND SPECIAL ABILITIES

Lotus 1-2-3, WordPerfect 5.1, 6.0 and Microsoft Word. IBM and Macintosh computers, printers, fax, adding machines and copiers. Courteous and helpful. Organized, dedicated and eager to learn.

EMPLOYMENT HISTORY

1993-1994	**ASSISTANT,** Esson Gas, San Francisco	
1991-1992	**ACCOUNTING/DATA ENTRY CLERK,** Star Taxi, Sacramento	
1990-1991	**COMPUTER OPERATOR,** Confederation Trust Company, Sacramento	

EDUCATION

1994	**OFFICE SKILLS PROGRAM,** Careers First Business College	
1992	**CAREER DEVELOPMENT WORKSHOP,** Somerset College	

References Available Upon Request

> Cheryl's second "After" resume is tailored to her second job choice of a Secretary/Office Clerk. Notice how the order of her work experience is shifted to emphasize relevant "office support" duties first. Cheryl's new tailored approach proved to be a winner—it helped her get the job she wanted.

CHERYL BENSON
44 Cedar Hill Street, San Francisco, CA 10002   *(123) 555-0244*

Secretary/Office Clerk

QUALIFICATIONS

Four years' varied experience in the clerical field including data entry/ accounting positions. Thorough knowledge of office procedures with excellent computer skills and accurate keyboarding abilities. Work well under pressure. Good public relations skills. Very dependable and hardworking.

RELEVANT EXPERIENCE

OFFICE SUPPORT:

- Typed and edited letters and memos using a word processor.
- Answered and redirected incoming calls and recorded messages.
- Handled inquiries regarding accounts and reassured customers.
- Filed and maintained statements, company and customer records.
- Photocopied letters, memos, coupons and statements.
- As an Assistant for Esson: purchased goods and supplies, maintained store room and equipment inventory, handled temporary and permanent staff scheduling, collected car wash vouchers, calculated totals for accountant and effectively prioritized tasks.

PUBLIC RELATIONS:

- As Accounting Clerk for Star Taxi, regularly handled complaints and helped satisfy customers by locating source of monthly statement errors and bringing them to manager's attention.
- Consistently tended to all customer problems and needs and was very helpful to drivers, staff and coworkers.

ACCOUNTING/DATA ENTRY:

- Performed weekly accounting procedures for accounts receivable/payable using computerized systems.
- Prepared, verified and issued monthly billing statements, and balanced monthly cash flow transactions.
- As Accounting Clerk with Star Taxi, processed route orders of hundreds of drivers and consistently verified their accuracy with dispatchers.

TECHNICAL SKILLS AND SPECIAL ABILITIES

Lotus 1-2-3, WordPerfect 5.1, 6.0 and Microsoft Word. IBM and Macintosh computers, printers, fax, adding machines and copiers. Courteous and helpful. Organized, dedicated and eager to learn.

EMPLOYMENT HISTORY

1993-1994	**ASSISTANT,** Esson Gas, San Francisco
1991-1992	**ACCOUNTING/DATA ENTRY CLERK,** Star Taxi, Sacramento
1990-1991	**COMPUTER OPERATOR,** Confederation Trust Company, Sacramento

EDUCATION

1994	**OFFICE SKILLS PROGRAM,** Careers First Business College
1992	**CAREER DEVELOPMENT WORKSHOP,** Somerset College

References Available Upon Request

Harriet Landsbury
73 Crystal Drive
Cleveland, Ohio 10002
(123) 555-6823

Harriet has a lot more to offer than her resume reveals. Her Job History is all bones with no meat, and her Objective is too vague. Because Harriet was interested in two positions, we formed two separate resumes, tailored to each job.

Objective:

Needs a clear, specific Objective.

Clerical position, utilizing my office experience, my newly attained skills obtained at Western College, with opportunity for advancement.

Qualifications:

People Skills
- 10 years' experience meeting customer needs
- Ability to please customers under all circumstances
- Cheerful personality
- Bilingual in oral French and able to read French fluently.

Office Skills
- Typing 40 words per minute
- Familiar with WordPerfect 5.1, Lotus 1-2-3, Simply Accounting, Accpac Plus
- Knowledgeable about office procedures

Employment:

Staffers Temporary Agency	Cleveland, Ohio
General Clerk	1984 to 1985
Union Life	Cincinnati, Ohio
Accounting Clerk	1971 to 1983
Venture Travel	Cleveland, Ohio
Advertisement Clerk	1983 to 1984
Glenwood Bank of Commerce	230 Reed Avenue
Human Resources Clerk	1985 to 1992

Emphasize jobs and duties relevant to a specific objective

Education:

Western College   Cleveland, Ohio

Certificate Operation Office Systems   1994-1995

Hawthorne College, Cleveland, Ohio, North Campus
Vocational Orientation & Updating Academic Skills   1993-1994

Delta University   Ohio
Letter of Accomplishment (Bank Assoc.)
-       1. Introduction to Business Organization   Simplify Education section.
-       2. Interpersonal Communication
-       3. Organizational Behavior

References

Available upon request

Powerful job descriptions make Harriet shine as an exceptional candidate. With the help of the Functional Style format, we positioned her most relevant customer service duties first. Now, everything is geared toward the specific job she is applying for.

HARRIET LANDSBURY
73 Crystal Drive
Cleveland, Ohio 10002
(123) 555-6823

Customer Service Clerk

QUALIFICATIONS

Twenty years of clerical experience involving high level of public contact. Excellent customer relations skills. Extremely dedicated to job and customers. Cheerful individual with accurate keyboarding abilities. Newly upgraded computer skills.

WORK EXPERIENCE

AS A MORTGAGE RENEWAL CLERK:

- Answered over 100 incoming calls per day. Solely handled all inquiries from customers and bank branches regarding renewal agreements and rates.
- Pleased customers under all circumstances:
  - Patiently dealt with irate customers.
  - Discussed mortgage concerns and explained benefits of mortgage payments.
  - On occasion, personally delivered mortgage forms from customers' homes to bank.
- Performed all duties promptly and efficiently - renewed mortgages on computer, verified codes and rates, and processed checks.
- Ran monthly meetings and presentations on how to improve department.
- Handled many tasks simultaneously.
- Always helped cheer fellow coworkers.

AS A HUMAN RESOURCES CLERK:

- Answered calls from offices all across the U.S. regarding employee accounts.
- Handled files of employees transferred to new job locations.
- Set up employee bank accounts in head office.
- Recorded all salary and moving information in log books.
- Monitored employee salaries and verified expense figures on computer.
- Formulated and typed letters and correspondence.

Special Achievement:

- Awarded three Perfect Attendance Certificates (punctuality and no absenteeism for two consecutive years).

AS AN ACCOUNTING CLERK:

- Handled health, dental and life insurance accounts.
- Balanced accounts with bank statements.
- Followed up on outstanding checks or other items. Brought any errors to manager's attention.
- Provided proper bank statements to auditors at year end.
- Worked overtime or helped other departments when needed.

Employer Comment:

"Always willing to do above and beyond her duties. Very flexible and approachable."

TECHNICAL SKILLS AND SPECIAL ABILITIES

- Lotus 1-2-3, Advanced Lotus, Lotus Version 5 (self-taught), AccPac Plus, Simply Accounting, WordPerfect 5.1, Microsoft Word.
- Bookkeeping, advanced math, fast numeric keyboard skills.
- HP copier, fax, image processing machine, IBM computers (can work from mainframe), LAN printers.
- Spreadsheets, graphs, enhanced graph worksheets.
- Efficient, goal-oriented and very committed.

LANGUAGES

Bilingual - English/French

EMPLOYMENT HISTORY

1991-1992	HUMAN RESOURCES CLERK, Glenwood Bank, Cleveland
1985-1991	MORTGAGE RENEWAL CLERK, Glenwood Bank, Cleveland
1984-1985	GENERAL CLERK, Staffers Temporary Agency, Cleveland
1983-1984	ADVERTISEMENT CLERK, Venture Travel, Cleveland
1971-1983	ACCOUNTING CLERK, Union Life, Cincinnati

EDUCATION

1994-1995	CERTIFICATE OPERATION OFFICE SYSTEMS, Western College
1993-1994	VOCATIONAL ORIENTATION AND UPDATING ACADEMIC SKILLS, Hawthorne College
1989-1990	BUSINESS AND COMMUNICATION COURSES, Delta University

References Available Upon Request

HARRIET LANDSBURY
73 Crystal Drive
Cleveland, Ohio 10002
(123) 555-6823

> Harriet's second "After" resume emphasizes accounting experience and skills to support her Accounting Clerk Job Objective. Notice that the order of her job positions and duties is shifted to emphasize her most relevant accounting experience first.

Accounting Clerk

QUALIFICATIONS

Extremely dedicated. Twenty years' experience with accounting/clerical positions. Newly upgraded computer skills. Accurate keyboarding. Exceptional math ability. Excellent customer relations skills. Methodical and detail-oriented.

WORK EXPERIENCE

AS AN ACCOUNTING CLERK:

- Handled all health, dental and life insurance accounts.
- Balanced accounts with bank statements.
- Followed up on outstanding checks or other items. Brought any errors to manager's attention.
- Provided proper bank statements to auditors at year end.
- Worked overtime or helped other departments when needed.

Employer Comment:

"Always willing to do above and beyond her duties. Very flexible and approachable."

AS A MORTGAGE RENEWAL CLERK:

- Renewed mortgages on computer. Verified computer codes and rates. Processed mortgage checks.
- Answered over 100 incoming calls per day. Solely handled all inquiries from customers and bank branches regarding renewal agreements and rates.
- Pleased customers under all circumstances:
  - Patiently dealt with irate customers.
  - Discussed mortgage concerns and explained benefits of mortgage payments.
- Ran monthly meetings and presentations on how to improve department.
- Performed all duties promptly and efficiently. Handled many tasks simultaneously.

AS A HUMAN RESOURCES CLERK:

- Handled files of employees transferred to new job locations.
- Set up employee bank accounts in head office.
- Recorded all salary and moving information into log books.
- Monitored employee salaries and verified expense figures on computer.
- Answered calls from offices all across the U.S. regarding employee accounts.
- Formulated and typed letters and correspondence.

Special Achievement:

- Awarded three Perfect Attendance Certificates (punctuality and no absenteeism for two consecutive years).

TECHNICAL SKILLS AND SPECIAL ABILITIES

- Lotus 1-2-3, Advanced Lotus, Lotus Version 5 (self-taught), AccPac Plus, Simply Accounting, Word-perfect 5.1, and Microsoft Word.
- Bookkeeping, advanced math, fast numeric keyboard skills.
- HP copier, fax, image processing machine, IBM computers (can work from mainframe), LAN printers.
- Spreadsheets, graphs, enhanced graph worksheets.
- Efficient, goal-oriented and very committed.

LANGUAGES

Bilingual - English/French

EMPLOYMENT HISTORY

1991-1992	HUMAN RESOURCES CLERK, Glenwood Bank, Cleveland
1985-1991	MORTGAGE RENEWAL CLERK, Glenwood Bank, Cleveland
1984-1985	GENERAL CLERK, Staffers Temporary Agency, Cleveland
1983-1984	ADVERTISEMENT CLERK, Venture Travel, Cleveland
1971-1983	ACCOUNTING CLERK, Union Life, Cincinnati

EDUCATION

1994-1995	CERTIFICATE OPERATION OFFICE SYSTEMS, Western College
1993-1994	VOCATIONAL ORIENTATION AND UPDATING ACADEMIC SKILLS, Hawthorne College
1989-1990	BUSINESS AND COMMUNICATION COURSES, Delta University

References Available Upon Request

RESUME

ROBERT MILLER
329 NORTH RIDGEWAY DRIVE
DENVER, COLORADO
(123) 555-6244

Robert is unfamiliar with modern resume writing. His "Before" resume is a long, generic listing of anything and everything he's ever learned or done, and he even forgets to include job titles. No employer would have a clue as to what he's after.

Needs a Job Objective and Summary of Qualifications.

EDUCATION

SEPT. 1988-MAY 1989   SUCCESS COLLEGE
181 Main Street
Denver, CO 10002
Ph# 555-6493

Position Education after Experience.

COURSES STUDIED:
Philosophy, Social Science,
Political Science, U.S. Economy
Entrepreneurics, Creative Thinking,
Science and Technology in Society

1984-1987   CENTRAL TECHNICAL AND COMMERCIAL SCHOOL
291 Shawnee Crescent
Denver, CO 10002

Simplify Education section.

COURSES STUDIED:
Auto Mechanics, Business Management,
Data Processing

OTHER COURSES

Conversational French at Success College and Collegiate.

Investment management at the University of Denver

Communications - Business, Letter Writing, Barton College

Auto mechanics, certificate in engines, electronic fuel injection and automobile electronics.

WORK EXPERIENCE

June 1989-Present   MANPOWER CENTER
4222 Bolton Avenue
Denver, CO 10002
Ph.# 555-2121

Detail positions relevant to a specific Job Objective.

DUTIES:
-Directing incoming calls to correct personnel.
-Directing the public to the appropriate departments of the Manpower Center.

April 88-July 88

Eliminate everything irrelevant.

HITECH SECURITY LTD.
65 Cowan Avenue East
Denver, CO 10002
Ph.# 555-9946

Duties:
-Patrolled and controlled access to assigned premises.
-Provided protection for clients and properties.
-Logged daily report of occurrences.

Jan.88 - Mar. 88

SMITH'S BOOKSTORE
490 Terrydale Street
Denver, CO
Ph.# 555-1673

Duties:
-Received and checked merchandise and invoices.
-Allocated merchandise to appropriate departments.
-Prepared invoices.
-Set up special displays.

May 87 - Aug. 87

CARLTON FILMS
77 Carlton Avenue
Denver, Colorado 10002
Ph.# 555-8268

Duties:
-Received purchase orders from customers by telephone
-Budget and allocate funds for shipping expenses.
-Filled out sorted and filed invoices
-Data entry on IBM XT Compatible

June 85 - May 86

MAXI SECURITY GUARDS LTD.
440 Dustin Street
Denver, CO 10002
Ph.# 555-0020

Duties:
-Patrolled and secured assigned premises
-Controlled incoming and outgoing traffic to restricted areas
-Monitored security alarm system
-Logged Reports of Daily Occurrences

Dec.85 - Feb. 87	BUTTERWORTH MACMILLAN ASSOCIATES 133 Forest Valley Road Suite 91 Denver, CO 10002 Ph.# 555-0774

Duties:
-Telephone number searcher
-Receptionist
-Office clerk

COMPUTER EXPERIENCE -Hands on experience with Apple Macintosh, IBM compatible and
IBM computers

OTHER EXPERIENCES
-Vice President of Student Council
-Photographer and Advertising editor for School Yearbook Committee
-Board of Education Student Representative
-Member of a Committee that organized Race Relations Conference
 at Central
-Assisted in the organization of a multi-cultural, leadership camp
 for high school students.
-Received an award for outstanding individual in the community
 from the Glenwood Afro-American Club.

SPECIAL INTERESTS   Photography, literature.

Robert's new, streamlined resume is geared toward Customer Service. His best abilities are presented, and job descriptions for his most relevant jobs are added and quantified. We even pulled together a list of technical skills he never thought he had.

ROBERT MILLER
329 North Ridgeway Drive, Denver CO 10002   (123) 555-6244

Customer Service Representative

SUMMARY OF QUALIFICATIONS:

Seven years' experience involving heavy client contact. Excellent oral communication skills and client relations. Extremely versatile - can undertake many different job functions with ease. Hardworking and goal-oriented.

WORK EXPERIENCE:

1989-Present - Manpower Center, Denver

CLIENT SERVICES REPRESENTATIVE

- Provided information on programs and services to employers, clients and the general public.
- Assisted 50-75 clients per day; answered queries and concerns, referred clients to suitable jobs and appropriate agencies.
- Effectively dealt with difficult or irate clients.
- Reviewed applications for unemployment and social security, maternity and parental benefits.
- Managed all monies - issued receipts, logged cash, handled accounting, deposits and reconciliations.
- Assumed additional job positions when necessary, e.g., handled switchboard - 200 calls per day.
- Responsible for all aspects of the department, from client assistance to petty cash to office security.

EMPLOYMENT OFFICER

- Determined client needs; referred clients to appropriate services and matched clients to suitable job vacancies.
- Assisted clients in completion of application forms.

ACTING SUPERVISOR

- Supervised 5-7 Client Service Representatives.
- Trained and motivated staff. Performed annual staff evaluations.
- Handled inquiries from governor's offices.
- Sat on management committees.
- Summarized and presented department concerns to management staff.

EDUCATION:

1995	SUCCESS COLLEGE, Auto Mechanics
1994	BARTON COLLEGE, Communications, Business Writing
1989-1990	UNIVERSITY OF DENVER, Investment Management
1990-1991	DRAKE UNIVERSITY, Philosophy
1984-1987	CENTRAL TECHNICAL AND COMMERCIAL SCHOOL, SSGD Diploma

TECHNICAL SKILLS AND SPECIAL ABILITIES:

WordPerfect 5.0, dBase and MacWrite. Apple and IBM computers, HP laser and dot matrix printers, switchboard, fax, copiers, electronic mail. Bondable. Mechanically inclined. Troubleshoot equipment. Problem solver. Thoroughly enjoy assisting individuals.

REFERENCES: Available Upon Request

Amanda's "Before" resume is mediocre at best. Her Job Objective is too vague, and she fails to elaborate on her recent relevant database job.

AMANDA STEVENS

59 Cherry Hill Street
Milwaukee, WI 10002

Res: **(123) 555-7440**
(123) 555-3298

OBJECTIVE: To utilize my skills and experience in business `Needs a specific Objective.`

SKILLS: Data entry skills
Organizational skills
Familiar with Microsoft Excel (Macintosh)
Proficient with Lotus 1-2-3

BUSINESS EXPERIENCE:

Mar. 1995 - Feb. 1996

INFONET - A COMPUTEL COMPANY
Downtown Milwaukee, WI
Database Steward

- Updating and maintenance of security cross reference files.

`Merge two database jobs into one. Add detailed job duties.`

Mar. 1992 - Mar. 1995

COMPUTEL INFORMATION SERVICES
Downtown Milwaukee, WI
Database Steward

- Updating and maintenance of security cross reference files.

1975-1992

CITY SHOPS, Milwaukee

Inventory Planning Control Clerk

- Compilation of the weekly reports on clothing style and department category performance; breaking down information to various levels for management and department directors.
- Input store sales data information.
- Followed up with stores' information if incomplete.
- Computing and balancing of weekly reports - unit tally and stock count.
- Input data for PC reports and produced information on manufacturers, department dates, colors, units and dollar purchases, as well as dollar receipts.

- Input data for special projects.
- Photocopied and distributed reports to management in a timely and efficient manner.

Worked as a Stock Control Clerk

- Sorting tickets and check-off counts on stock cards.
- Write up debit memos.
- Filed stock cards.
- Fill special orders for customers.

Worked in the Stores' Transfer Department as a Distribution Clerk

- Replenishment of merchandise for stores (all City Shops locations).

Worked as a Data Entry Operator

- Responsible for entering totals for bank reconciliations.

EDUCATION:

1964-1968   Saint Paul University, Philippines

Bachelor of Science
Teaching Certificate, Elementary School Level

INTERESTS: Avid reader

Enjoy meeting people | Omit interests. |

Interest in sewing and cooking

REFERENCES: Available upon request

Amanda's "After" resume is much sharper. Its professionalized layout, specific job objective, and compact but powerful job descriptions make her a strong candidate for the position she wants.

AMANDA STEVENS
59 Cherry Hill Street, Milwaukee, WI 10002   (123) 555-7440

DATA ENTRY OPERATOR

SUMMARY OF QUALIFICATIONS

- 20 years' experience in data entry and various clerical positions.
- Reliable, dedicated worker able to work with minimum supervision.
- Extremely accurate. Good computer skills. Easily trainable.

JOB HISTORY

1992-Present, Computel Information Services, Milwaukee

DATABASE STEWARD

Updated and maintained security cross reference files for this international trading company.

- Checked and corrected securities data including interest rates, maturity rates, names and descriptions of securities, existing cross references, ISIN numbers, market symbols and rate types.
- Accurately researched correct information using International Securities Identification Directory and monthly supplements.
- Worked continuously without taking breaks and without requiring supervision.
- Praised as a very devoted, hard worker by Director of Securities Services.

1975-1992 City Shops, Head Office, Milwaukee

DATA ENTRY OPERATOR

- Entered sales totals for bank reconciliations for 212 stores across the United States.

INVENTORY PLANNING CONTROL CLERK

- Accurately input clothing sales data - code, style, manufacturer, unit and selling price - on computer.
- Calculated totals of weekly stock count for 212 stores, and compiled weekly unit tally and cumulative reports for department directors.
- Handled customer inquiries in supervisor's absence.

Additional positions held at City Shops:

DISTRIBUTION CLERK
STOCK CONTROL CLERK

EDUCATION

1995	KEYBOARDING I, Milwaukee Secondary School, Milwaukee
1964-1968	BACHELOR OF SCIENCE, Saint Paul University, Philippines

TECHNICAL SKILLS

Software:	Lotus 1-2-3, Microsoft Excel, WordPerfect 5.1
Hardware:	IBM, NEC, Apple Macintosh, Compaq Presario
Equipment:	Fax, copiers, printers

REFERENCES AVAILABLE UPON REQUEST

> John's "Before" resume starts off with two huge paragraph chunks that make his resume difficult to plow through. His Job Objective says "me, me, me," and his Summary unnecessarily repeats duties from the resume.

JOHN LEWIS

4020 Carter Street
Apartment No. 517
Los Angeles, CA 10002   Tele:(123) 555-4118

OBJECTIVES:

Needs a clear, simple Objective.

To be able to utilize my skills in a major Data Processing environment. To challenge my abilities by exposing myself to new and varied environments. To upgrade my technical skills and abilities by undergoing as much technical training as possible, thereby positioning myself for an eventual jump in my career.

SUMMARY

Scale down Summary.

Over 20 years of experience in Statistical and Data Processing environment in one of the largest Research and Development organizations in Bombay, India. Responsibilities included design, collection, compilation and analysis of resources data, statistical interpretation of data and preparation of scientific papers. Headed the computer and statistics cell and have proficiency in Oracle RDBMS, Unix and DOS. Hold Masters Degree in Mathematics with Statistics and Post Graduate Diploma in Computer Management. Attended international job-related training programs.

EXPERIENCE:

October 1995-
Present

Tele-Prospecting,
Investors of America, Los Angeles

Major Tasks:
Contacted an exclusive set of customers, who include top executives of large companies worldwide, surveyed their requirements vis-à-vis the company's product.

May 1994-
July 1995

Statistician, Ocean Surveys of India, Bombay, India

Use Functional Style format to position relevant jobs first.

Major Tasks:
-Designed, collected and analyzed resources data.
-Introduced statistical tools for interpretation of data.
-Designed and implemented library management system.
-Upgraded the data processing environment from DOS to Unix and Oracle RDBMS.
-Selected appropriate software, installation and training of users.
-Database Administrator for Unix and Oracle.
-Headed the Computer and Statistics Cell.

| June 1991-
May 1994 | Junior Statistician/Data Processing Assistant
Ocean Surveys of India, Bombay, India |

Major Tasks:
-Collected and processed resources data.
-Planned, evaluated and monitored the survey cruises of institute research
 vessels.
-Published 12 scientific papers.

| June 1986-
May 1994 | Computer Programmer, Ocean Surveys of India, Bombay |

Major Tasks:
-Designed and implemented Resources Management System, Personnel Man-
 agement System and Inventory Control.
-Introduced Computers into the Organization.
-Selected appropriate software, installed and trained users.
-Responsible for Data entry through a team of Data Entry Operators.

SKILLS

Operating System: Unix, DOS.
Data Base Systems: Oracle RDBMS, dbase.
PC Skills: WordPerfect, Lotus dbase.
Communication Software: Radix.

EDUCATION:

Masters Degree in Mathematics with Statistics, University of India.
Diploma in Computer Management, University of India, India

TRAINING:

Trained in Statistical Data Collection conducted by The Development School,
Bangkok, Thailand.
Trained in Software Programming for processing of Data by the Institute of
Oceans, Tromso, Norway
Trained in Stock Assessment conducted by MORRISON TECH.

REFERENCES:

Will be furnished on request.

JOHN LEWIS
4020 Carter Street, #517, Los Angeles, CA

(123) 555-4118

OBJECTIVE

Data Processor

John's "After" resume contains a clear Job Objective and easier-to-read Summary. We formed his Job History in the Functional Style to omit his recent telemarketing job and focus on relevant data processing ones instead.

SUMMARY

- Twenty years' experience in statistical and data processing.
- Proficient with several operating and database systems.
- Hold Masters Degree in mathematics with statistics and diploma in computer management.

EXPERIENCE

AS A DATA PROCESSOR/STATISTICIAN:

Processed information for one of the largest national research and development organizations in India.
- Collected, analyzed and processed resources data.
- Introduced statistical tools for interpretation of data.
- Upgraded the data processing environment from DOS to Unix and Oracle RDBMS.
- Developed and installed appropriate software and trained 50 users.
- Designed and implemented the library management system.
- Acted as Database Administrator for Unix and Oracle.
- Headed the Computer and Statistics Cell.
- Planned, evaluated and monitored the survey cruises of institute research vessels.
- Prepared and published 12 scientific papers on fisheries and statistical applications.

AS A COMPUTER PROGRAMMER:

- Introduced computers to the organization - selected and installed appropriate software and trained users.
- Designed and implemented various software programs including Resources Management System, Personnel Management System and Inventory Control.

TECHNICAL SKILLS

Operating systems: Unix, DOS
Database systems: Oracle RDBMS, dbase
PC skills: WordPerfect, Lotus, dbase
Communication software: Radix

EMPLOYMENT HISTORY

1995-now	TELEMARKETER, Investors of America, Los Angeles
1991-1995	DATA PROCESSOR, Ocean Surveys of India, Bombay
1986-1994	COMPUTER PROGRAMMER, Ocean Surveys of India, Bombay

EDUCATION AND TRAINING

1992	STOCK ASSESSMENT, Morrison Tech, Bombay
1989	SOFTWARE PROGRAMMING, Institute of Oceans, Tromso, Norway
1988	STATISTICAL DATA COLLECTION, The Development School, Bangkok
1980	COMPUTER MANAGEMENT DIPLOMA, University of India
1971-1973	MASTERS DEGREE, MATH WITH STATISTICS, University of India

REFERENCES AVAILABLE UPON REQUEST

Laura's "Before" resume is already in the Functional Style to hide problem job dates. Though it is nice, it still doesn't sell her as effectively as it could. Her main problem is that her functional experience section lumps all duties together without job or category divisions.

LAURA PETERSON

9023 Fork Avenue, Apt. 8370
Tulsa, OK 10002
(123) 555-4669

Career Objective: Bookkeeping/Accounting Position

HIGHLIGHTS OF QUALIFICATIONS

* Over 10 years' experience in Accounting
* Can adapt immediately to any Accounting System
* Computer literate: Accpac Plus, Bedford I and II, Lotus 1-2-3, W.P. 5.1, dBase, Windows, Symphony
* Exceptionally responsible, diligent and thorough
* Dedicated to professionalism, highly motivated toward goal achievement
* Able to work well independently with minimal supervision or with or as part of a team

RELEVANT EXPERIENCE

Divide duties according to jobs or category.

* Organized diverse work load effectively ensuring tight deadlines were met
* Performed A/P and A/R duties for Trust and General Bank accounts
* Made and posted adjusting entries in General Ledger
* Reconciled numerous Bank Accounts
* Administered and scheduled Trust Accounts Deposits to secure maximum return for clients
* Calculated and reconciled management staff remuneration
* Balanced and deposited daily cash flow
* Oversaw payroll functions including tax deductions and health benefits
* Performed manual and computerized check runs
* Designed computer programs utilizing INFO / ACCESS language
* Provided assistance with special projects

WORK HISTORY

1991 - 1996	**Freelance and Contract Work**	Independent Consulting Services	"Freelance work" too vague. List specific jobs for this recent 5-year period.
1989 - 1991	**Accounting Clerk**	Homestar Realty Ltd., Tulsa	
1985 - 1989	**Accounts Payable Clerk**	Murphy Williams, Tulsa	
1982 - 1985	**Bookkeeper**	Layton Enterprises Ltd., Tulsa	
1980 - 1982	**Accounting Clerk**	Modern Drapery, Oklahoma City	

EDUCATION

Add dates.

Computer Applications Diploma
Johnson Computer College, Tulsa

Accounting Course
The Business Academy, Oklahoma City

REFERENCES AVAILABLE UPON REQUEST

Laura's "After" resume, still in the Functional Style, groups duties according to job to make it clearer for the reader. Quantified job descriptions show the extent of her work, and a positive employer comment gives her resume a shot of personality that makes it stand out from the rest.

LAURA PETERSON
9023 Fork Avenue, #8370
Tulsa, OK 10002
(123) 555-4669

BOOKKEEPER

SUMMARY OF QUALIFICATIONS

Highly capable, resourceful individual with excellent problem-solving abilities. 16 years' accounting experience. Can immediately adapt to any accounting system. Organized, accurate and detail-oriented.

WORK EXPERIENCE

BOOKKEEPING/ACCOUNTING:

At Classic Jewelers Head Office

- Handled huge workloads - reconciled and processed all invoices and followed up on thousands of outstanding credit notes and claims.
- Interacted with Inventory Control Department, buyers, suppliers and 200 store locations across the U.S.
- Trained salespeople and managers to process claims and inventory on new automated systems.
- Handled duties above and beyond official job description - became the troubleshooter for any and all problems.

At Homestar Realty Head Office

- Handled accounts receivable/payable, insurance benefits, trust accounts and bank reconciliations for all accounts.
- Calculated payroll deductions for a support staff of 35 and processed government remittances for 200 staff members.
- Calculated and adjusted sales commissions for management staff of six.
- Balanced and deposited daily cash flow.
- Effectively prioritized workloads.
- Consistently met all deadlines - appraised by manager as having a "steely determination to finish work despite any obstacles or circumstances."

COMPUTER SKILLS

AccPac Plus 6.1, Lotus 1-2-3, Windows Excel, dBase, Bedford I and II, WordPerfect 5.1 and Symphony.

EMPLOYMENT HISTORY

1994-1996	**ACCOUNTING CLERK,** Classic Jewelers, Tulsa
1989-1991	**ACCOUNTING/ADMINISTRATION CLERK,** Homestar Realty, Tulsa
1985-1989	**ACCOUNTS PAYABLE CLERK,** Murphy Williams Ltd., Tulsa
1982-1985	**BOOKKEEPER,** Layton Enterprises, Tulsa
1980-1982	**ACCOUNTING CLERK,** Modern Drapery, Oklahoma City

EDUCATION

1991-1992	**ACCOUNTING SYSTEMS,** National College, Tulsa
1983-1984	**COMPUTER APPLICATIONS DIPLOMA,** Johnson Computer College, Tulsa
1979	**ACCOUNTING COURSE,** The Business Academy, Oklahoma City

REFERENCES AVAILABLE UPON REQUEST

VIVIAN CLARK
278 Orchard Park Road
Phoenix, Arizona 10002
(123) 555-7248

Vivian, a recent new grad, has some relevant experience working as a medical secretary two hours per week. However, she gives her resume that typical "inexperienced new grad" look by emphasizing Education and positioning it first.

Needs a Job Objective and Summary of Qualifications.

EDUCATION

1994-1996   **HORIZONS BUSINESS COLLEGE**
Phoenix, Arizona

Position Education after Experience.

Office Administration - Medical Diploma Program
Graduated in March 1996

Program of Study

Keyboarding (Type 50 w.p.m.)
WordPerfect 5.1 (Advanced Level)
Medical Terminology
Medical Machine Transcription
Filing
Applied Bookkeeping Practice

Turn course subjects into skills.

Medical Insurance Billing
Anatomy
Medical Office Procedures
Office Language Skills
English
Liberal Studies

1991-1994   **WILLOWBROOK HIGH SCHOOL**
Phoenix, Arizona

Secondary School Graduation Diploma
Grade 12

OTHER SKILLS

Good Communication Skills
Excellent Accuracy
Good Organizational Skills
Lotus 1-2-3
MS Word for Windows 2.0

EMPLOYMENT EXPERIENCE

August 1996   **Medical Secretary**
to Present   Duties: Answering telephones, booking appointments, filing, photocopying, taking patients in, booking appointments with specialists for patients, opening mail, confirming

Professionalize job duties.

patients about their appointments, and filling requisition forms.

Dr. MacMillan
Phoenix, Arizona

ACHIEVEMENT

Award - Outstanding Achievement in Science while in high school

Move award to
Education section.

INTERESTS

Omit interests.

Like to work with people
Working on computers
Traveling

REFERENCES

Available on request

Here we effectively played up Vivian's limited work experience, turned her course subjects into an impressive array of technical skills, and tailored her Qualifications Summary to an employer's specific needs to make this resume generate several interviews and a job offer.

VIVIAN CLARK
278 Orchard Park Road
Phoenix, Arizona 10002
(123) 555-7248

JOB OBJECTIVE

A medical secretarial position

SUMMARY OF QUALIFICATIONS

Experienced medical secretary. Honors graduate of a Medical Office Administration Program. Exceptional word processing abilities. Good organizational skills. Extremely accurate, hardworking and very reliable.

EMPLOYMENT EXPERIENCE

1996-Present   ***MEDICAL SECRETARY***
Dr. Jason MacMillan, Phoenix

- Answered large volume of incoming calls - dealt with patient inquiries and concerns, recorded and relayed messages.
- Booked and confirmed specialist and patient appointments.
- Handled busy patient flow - registered new patient data on computer, prepared files and guided patients to examining rooms.
- Filed large volume of patient charts and lab reports using an alphabetical filing system.
- Taught employer and office staff how to operate newly acquired Windows word processing software.
- Completed health forms and lab and x-ray requisitions.
- Photocopied various reports and forms. Opened and sorted mail.

EDUCATION

1994 - 1996   ***MEDICAL OFFICE ADMINISTRATION PROGRAM***
Graduated with Honors
Horizons Business College, Phoenix

1991 - 1994   ***SECONDARY SCHOOL HONOR GRADUATION DIPLOMA***
Award - Outstanding Achievement in Science
Willowbrook High School, Phoenix

TECHNICAL SKILLS AND SPECIAL ABILITIES

- Excellent knowledge of WordPerfect 5.1 (Advanced Level).
- Familiar with WordPerfect 5.2 & 6.0, MS Word for Windows 2.0 and Lotus 1-2-3.
- Excellent bookkeeping skills, medical machine transcription, medical terminology, computer and manual insurance billing, keyboarding 50 w.p.m.
- Operate laser printers, fax machines, photocopiers, electronic memory telephones, answering machines.
- Possess pleasant telephone manner.
- Very supportive of others.

REFERENCES AVAILABLE UPON REQUEST

RESUME

Jennifer, a graphic artist and teacher, looks as if she lacks experience for a reception job. That's because she doesn't know how to relate her previous job experience to her current Job Objective.

Jennifer Dayton
51 Eastman Crescent
Seattle, Washington 10002
(123) 555-9339

<u>JOB OBJECTIVE</u>: Receptionist

Needs a Summary of Qualifications.

<u>JOB HISTORY</u>

1980-1981 **GRAPHIC ARTIST**
VPR Graphics, Seattle, Washington

- Designed company logos.
- Worked on layout and type specifications.
- Created new designs and formats for sports catalogs, furniture catalogs, window covering brochures, etc.
- Layout and paste-up artist.
- Worked in cooperation with typesetters and lithographers.

Use Functional Style format to reorganize Job History.

1981-1983 **GRAPHIC ARTIST**
Self-employed

- Designed logos, brochures, flyers for companies, invitations, business cards and letterhead and envelopes.

1983-Present **READING TUTOR/TEACHER**
(Private)
- Improved children's reading skills ages 6-12.
- Administered reading tests to determine reading level.
- Reviewed students' educational background to determine whether past or present learning disabilities exist.
- Devised special educational methods that students would use as a learning tool.
- Met with 25-30 students per week for individual tutoring.
- Taught students with severe learning disabilities.
- Provided parents with analysis of students' progress and development.
- Set out rules and regulations that students had to live up to, e.g., taking responsibility for homework and practice follow-up.

Jennifer Dayton
Page 2

1974-1978 (During high school)	**ARTS AND CRAFTS/CROCHETING AND KNITTING TEACHER**
	- Taught classes of 15-25 students.

EDUCATION

1979-1980	**COLLEGE OF ART** Studio and storyboard illustration
	SMITH'S COLLEGE Oil Painting Credit Course
1978	**TRAINING COLLEGE FOR TEACHERS** Teaching methodology, psychology, history, English
	ART CORRESPONDENCE COURSE During high school
	YEARBOOK ARTIST (For Junior High and High School Annual Yearbook)
	(and artist for school's fundraising dinner)

SKILLS

- Excellent rapport with children and parents.
- Very polite.
- Organized.
- Fostered new clients through other satisfied parents - parents used to say I did wonderful job with their kids.

Pull out skills relevant to reception job.

Jennifer Dayton
51 Eastman Crescent, Seattle, Washington 10002   **(123) 555-9339**

Job Objective

Receptionist or Entry Level Secretarial position

Summary of Qualifications

- Excellent public relations and oral communication skills.
- Familiar with WordPerfect 5.1. Well-organized problem solver.
- Extremely willing to learn and eager to build an office career.

Relevant Experience

PUBLIC RELATIONS:

- As a Reading Tutor, established excellent rapport with students and parents.
- Provided information regarding programs offered.
- Dealt with parent concerns and inquiries and discussed student progress.
- Patiently handled any complaints objectively and fairly.
- Fostered new customers through existing satisfied parents.
- As a Graphic Artist, interviewed and assisted company presidents; determined their needs and requirements.
- Worked in cooperation with typesetters, printers and lithographers on a daily basis.

SCHEDULING AND ORGANIZING:

- Booked and monitored appointments for 30 students per week.
- Maintained detailed and accurate records of student progress and homework.
- Filed student records using an alphabetical system.
- Planned educational programs according to students' abilities.
- Met deadlines for printing brochures and flyers.

CLERICAL/ADMINISTRATIVE:

- At VPR Graphics, provided reception relief for President and Vice President - answered phones, took messages, and typed letters.
- Purchased graphic art supplies, equipment and materials.
- As a Tutor, collected monies, made bank deposits and followed up on outstanding bills.

Technical Skills and Special Abilities

Operate fax, copiers, typewriters, calculators, answering machines. Excellent graphic design. Good listener. Polite. Extremely accurate and hardworking.

Employment History

1983-Present	READING TUTOR/TEACHER, private
1981-1983	GRAPHIC ARTIST, self-employed
1980-1981	GRAPHIC ARTIST, VPR Graphics, Seattle, Washington

Education

1979-1980	STUDIO AND STORYBOARD ILLUSTRATION, College of Art
1978	ENGLISH AND TEACHING METHODS, Training College for Teachers
1974-1978	TYPING AND OFFICE SKILLS, Fairview High School

References Available Upon Request

Jennifer's "After" resume has a whole new feel. Using the Functional Style format, we dug up and grouped together relevant duties from her irrelevant jobs and added appropriate functional headings—a truly innovative method that allows Jennifer's resume to compete with all the rest!

Ellen has been out of the workforce for twenty years, which immediately gets revealed on her resume. She feels she doesn't have much to contribute, and it shows.

ELLEN GREY
465 Summit Valley Drive
Richmond, Virginia 10002
TEL: (123) 555-2448

Add a Job Objective and Summary of Qualifications.

Job History:

Aug. 71-76   Senior Group Ratings Clerk
                  Mutual Life Insurance Co.

As a Senior Group Ratings Clerk, I was responsible for rating and checking group rates for quotations, new businesses, renewals. I was supervising the smooth operation of the rating pool and getting out all policies on time.

Oct. 69-70   Sales Audit Clerk

Use functional style format to camouflage dates.

                  Wingdale's Department Stores

Balanced cash register receipts with the computer sheets.

Nov. 66-70   Checker in the Typing Pool
                  International Surveys Ltd

Checked the amount and percentage of products sold.

Provided detailed job duties.

61-63   Office Clerk
                  Financial Collection Agency

Supervising the filing and mailings of the company.

60-61   Claimant's Interviewer
                  Unemployment Insurance Center

Checking the claimant's eligibility for getting their benefits. Also interviewing and interpreting.

Education:

Business School - Grade 12, Norfolk, 1956
Business Machines - Eastview Secondary School, 67
Bookkeeping - Adult Education Center, Completed Grade 10 of government course.
Introductory Computer course - Fosters School 1995

Add a Skills section.

We formed Ellen's new resume in the Functional Style to focus on her impressive past experience and deemphasize her old job dates. We worked hard to pull out her strongest relevant features and abilities, and even discovered some office equipment skills she never realized she had.

ELLEN GREY
465 Summit Valley Drive, Richmond, VA 10002   (123) 555-2448

JOB OBJECTIVE:

Position as a Financial Clerk.

SUMMARY OF QUALIFICATIONS:

Sixteen years of financial clerical experience. Highly dependable, conscientious individual eager to re-start career. Superb mathematical abilities. Fast numeric keyboard skills. Quick, intelligent and hardworking.

WORK EXPERIENCE:

AS A SENIOR GROUP RATINGS CLERK:

- Calculated rates for life, medical and disability insurance.
- Provided quotations for group rates, new business and renewals.
- Supervised rating pool of four clerks, verified accuracy of calculations.
- Renewed all group policies on computer; obtained policyholder information, completed renewal rate calculations and forwarded to Underwriter for review.
- Maintained renewal filing system and updated record information.
- Maintained accurate logbooks.
- Compiled and prepared weekly production, follow-up and business reports.
- Performed general clerical duties - filed, distributed all incoming mail.
- Worked with accuracy and speed and performed well under pressure.
- Consistently evaluated by Underwriting Manager as an excellent employee.

AS A SALES AUDIT CLERK:

- Balanced daily cash register intake of 17 Wingdale stores across Richmond.
- Matched receipts to computer printout, located cashier errors and presented to Audit Department Supervisor.

AS AN OFFICE CLERK:

- Supervised the filing and mailings of the company.
- Proofread typed reports of figures for accuracy.

OFFICE EQUIPMENT:

Familiar with computers, business machines, calculators, electronic memory telephones, photocopiers, mailing machines, some switchboard.

EMPLOYMENT HISTORY:

1971-1976	SENIOR GROUP RATINGS CLERK, Mutual Life Assurance Co, Richmond
1969-1970	SALES AUDIT CLERK, Wingdale's Department Stores, Richmond
1966-1970	CHECKER, International Surveys Ltd, Richmond
1961-1963	OFFICE CLERK, Financial Collection Agency, Richmond
1960-1961	CLAIMANTS' INTERVIEWER, Unemployment Insurance Center, Richmond

EDUCATION:

1995	INTRODUCTORY COMPUTERS, Foster's Computer School, Richmond
1968	BOOKKEEPING COURSE, Adult Education Center, Richmond
1967	BUSINESS MACHINES, Eastview Secondary School, Richmond
1956	BUSINESS COURSES - GRADE 12, Business School, Norfolk

REFERENCES AVAILABLE UPON REQUEST

Gordon has been both an office manager and a clerk. He jumbles all his work experience into one resume that doesn't sell him very well. His managerial jobs make him look overqualified as a clerk, and his clerk jobs give the appearance that he's gone down in job level. What Gordon needs is two separate, tightly focused resumes, one for each position.

RESUME

Gordon Shaw
24 Grant Street, #367
Detroit, Michigan 10002

Telephone Number (123) 555-4099

Needs a Job Objective.

Summary of Business Experience:

All my business and administrative experience has been in financial institutions. As an administrator I supervised clerical staff; responsible for small branch administrative operations; hired and trained office staff; assisted with agent training; extensive relations with the general public and insurance brokers.

Gear Summary to a specific Objective.

EMPLOYMENT RECORD

1990-May '94   Statistics Center
                35 Fairway Avenue
                Detroit, Michigan 10002

                Processing Clerk

1987-1989   Records Clerk
                Veterans Affairs
                1112 Rose Avenue
                Detroit, Michigan 10002

                Emphasize jobs relevant to a specific Objective.

1977-1987   Policy Service Clerk
                Safeway Life Insurance Company
                Detroit, Michigan 10002

                Duties: Processing loans and surrenders; death claims, answering policy
                         holder correspondence.

1971-1974   Department Supervisor (Head Office)
                National Life Insurance Company
                Detroit, Michigan

                Duties: Contact with company branch offices; advising and consulting on policy service
                         enquiries; supervision of six clerical staff; compilation of daily measurement re-
                         ports and miscellaneous reports as required by the Policy Service Manager.

1967-1971   Office Manager (Branch Office)
                National Life Insurance Company
                Chicago, Illinois

Duties: Responsible for hiring and training of office staff; assisting with agent training; answering Head Office correspondence and letters from policyholders;
completion of financial reports for agents and worked with brokers on individual application for life insurance.

Streamline unorganized format.

I undertook special projects as directed by the Branch Manager and in addition I sold and serviced insurance on a selected basis.

1964-1967   Office Manager (Branch Office)
National Life Insurance Company
Sacramento, California

Duties: Similar to those outlined above.

1961-1964   Assistant Office Manager (Branch Office)
National Life Insurance Company
Montreal, Que.

Duties: Similar to the above and provided me with a training period to familiarize
me with Canadian methods.

1956-1961   During this period I received my initial training with National Life in Minneapolis.

EDUCATION

1950-1954   Metcalfe Regional High School
Minneapolis, Minnesota
Graduated 1954.

1954   Banking course, Carleton Bank
Minneapolis, Minnesota

1970   Life Office Management Association Institute
Principles of Life Insurance - Part 1
Graduated July 1970.

various dates Inter-company insurance courses

OTHER INTERESTS   Omit interests.

Antique clock collecting and restoring.
Treasurer of St. Mary's Support Group for the Widowed.

References available upon request.

GORDON SHAW
24 Grant Street, #367
Detroit, Michigan 10002
(123) 555-4099

For Gordon's first "After" resume, we focused on his recent clerk jobs and deemphasized his managerial positions to make him look just right as an office clerk.

JOB OBJECTIVE:

Office Clerk

SUMMARY OF QUALIFICATIONS:

- Clerical and administrative experience in financial institutions.
- Excellent interpersonal skills - extensive relations with the general public.
- Basic computer knowledge and data entry skills.
- Good oral and written communication skills. Very meticulous and organized.

RELEVANT EXPERIENCE:

1990-1994 **PROCESSING CLERK**
Statistics Center, Detroit, Michigan

- Processed hundreds of survey forms per day from across the U.S. regarding education, housing, travel and gun control.
- Verified accuracy and completeness of all questionnaires.

1987-1989 **RECORDS CLERK**
Veterans Affairs, Detroit, Michigan

- Monitored all incoming and outgoing records of the central filing system.
- Swiftly dispatched requisitioned files to various departments.
- Recorded file identification numbers on computer.
- Accurately matched unidentified correspondence to file numbers.

1977-1987 **POLICY SERVICE CLERK**
Safeway Life Insurance Company, Detroit

- Processed loans, surrenders, and death claims.
- Answered policyholder correspondence - researched information and calculated values.
- Sent memos to outside insurance agents.

1961-1977 Held supervisory and managerial positions with National Life Insurance Company at different branches throughout North America.

EDUCATION:

1970 PRINCIPLES OF LIFE INSURANCE, Life Office Management Association
1954 BANKING COURSE, Carleton Bank, Minneapolis

OFFICE EQUIPMENT:

Apple computers. Fax. Printers. Pitney Bowes copier. Some data entry.

REFERENCES:

Available upon request

GORDON SHAW
24 Grant Street, #367
Detroit, Michigan 10002
(123) 555-4099

JOB OBJECTIVE:

Office Manager

For Gordon's second "After" resume, to make him look impressive as an office manager, we used a Functional Style format to emphasize his managerial positions while deemphasizing old job dates and his irrelevent clerk jobs.

SUMMARY OF QUALIFICATIONS:

- Extensive administrative experience in financial institutions.
- Excellent interpersonal skills - extensive relations with the general public.
- Ability to supervise, hire and train office staff.
- Good oral and written communication skills. Very meticulous and organized.

EMPLOYMENT EXPERIENCE:

Held supervisory and managerial positions with National Life Insurance Company for 18 years at different branches across North America:

AS AN OFFICE MANAGER:

- Hired and trained dozens of insurance clerks and office staff.
- Answered head office correspondence and letters from policyholders.
- Completed financial reports for agents.
- Worked with brokers on individual applications for life insurance.
- Assisted with insurance agent training - taught how to calculate premiums.
- Attended meetings with salespeople, apprised agents of changes in company policy forms.
- Sold and serviced insurance on a selected basis.
- Undertook special projects as directed by Branch Manager.

AS A DEPARTMENT SUPERVISOR:

- Supervised clerical staff of six.
- Advised and consulted on policy service inquiries from policyholders.
- Monitored and compiled daily statistical reports.
- Contacted company branch offices when necessary.

SPECIAL SKILLS:

Thoroughly familiar with life insurance policies. Basic computer knowledge. Some data entry. Operate Apple computers, printers, fax, Pitney Bowes copier.

EMPLOYMENT HISTORY:

1990-1994	PROCESSING CLERK, Statistics Center, Detroit
1987-1989	RECORDS CLERK, Veterans Affairs, Detroit
1977-1987	POLICY SERVICE CLERK, Safeway Life Insurance, Detroit
1971-1974	DEPARTMENT SUPERVISOR, National Life Insurance, Detroit
1967-1971	OFFICE MANAGER, National Life Insurance, Chicago
1964-1967	OFFICE MANAGER, National Life Insurance, Sacramento
1961-1964	ASSISTANT OFFICE MANAGER, National Life Insurance, Montreal

EDUCATION:

1970	PRINCIPLES OF LIFE INSURANCE, Life Office Management Association
1954	BANKING COURSE, Carleton Bank, Minneapolis

REFERENCES AVAILABLE UPON REQUEST

What a Difference!

That's it for our sample resumes. What a difference the "After" versions make! They have taken on a whole new feel. No longer are they all-purpose, generic resumes with skimpy listings of skills and weak job duties. They are now precisely targeted with clear job objectives, full skills summaries, and powerful, professional job descriptions. Also, all superfluous and space-wasting material such as irrelevant jobs and courses and unnecessary hobbies and interests were eliminated to make these resumes sharp, streamlined, and truly attention-getting.

Tailoring Your Whole Resume—The Key to Resume Success

Notice that the underlying theme throughout all the preceding resumes is tailoring—tailoring your resume to a specific position by focusing on your most relevant skills and experience for that job.

It's not just any one section that gets tailored: As you have seen, the tailoring aspect runs throughout the whole resume—from your Job Objective right through your Summary of Qualifications to your Job History. That's what successful resume writing is all about. Gear your whole resume to the job you want and doors to that job will open for you.

More to the Sample Resumes Than Meets the Eye—Still More Tips and Advice to Gain

Surely, analyzing these resumes and their commentaries has helped you form your own best resume. But there's even more to gain than you might have noticed. Read on for more tips and advice. Find out how to back up the claims you made in your Summary of Qualifications, how to make yourself look great even when you're not perfect, and how to modify your resume to fit any job position.

Prove What You Say You Are—How to Back Up Your Summary of Qualifications Throughout Your Resume

The Summary of Qualifications section is more important to your whole resume than you may realize. It is the foundation

167

upon which the rest of your resume is built. Once you have made certain claims about yourself in the Summary of Qualifications, you must prove they're true by backing them up throughout your resume.

Perhaps you remember being introduced to this basic idea in Chapters 2 and 3 when you were forming your Summary of Qualifications and organizing your job duties. Hopefully, you've already included job duties or points in your resume that prove the claims you made. In case you haven't, or if you just want to make sure you've done it correctly, let's look at exactly how it's done using our sample resumes.

How we backed up the claims of the sample resume candidates

In all of the sample resumes, we fully supported any claims made in the Summary of Qualifications. Let's analyze a few to see how:

1. Here is one particular claim from Harriet Landsbury's Summary of Qualifications (page 138):

   "Extremely dedicated to job and customers."

   We didn't put this in just to make her sound good. And we certainly wouldn't have claimed she's extremely anything unless we could prove it. We substantiated this claim in her Job History with the following job descriptions:

   "Worked overtime or helped other departments when needed."

   "...personally delivered mortgage forms from customers' homes to bank."

   "Awarded three Perfect Attendance Certificates (punctuality and no absenteeism for two consecutive years)."

   Now, if this doesn't show a dedicated employee, I don't know what does. Here we showed *how* she was dedicated to her job and customers, thus effectively proving her "dedication" claim.

   Here's another one of Harriet's claims:

   "Excellent customer relations skills."

   Again, we backed this up in her Job History with the following job description:

   "Pleased customers under all circumstances—patiently dealt with irate customers, discussed mortgage concerns and explained benefits of mortgage payments," etc.

Again, we showed *how* she provided excellent customer service, thus proving her "excellent customer relations skills" claim.

2. Here is one of Vivian Clark's Summary of Qualifications' claims (page 157):

"Exceptional word processing abilities."

We backed this up in Vivian's Job History with the following job description:

"Taught employer and office staff how to operate newly acquired Windows word processing software."

If I were the employer, I'd be convinced. Anyone who can teach word processing to others must be pretty darn good at it themselves. Now an employer can see that her claim to exceptional WP skills is true.

In addition, Vivian's word processing claim was supported even further, in her Technical Skills and Special Abilities, when we listed the following numerous programs she can operate:

"Excellent knowledge of WordPerfect 5.1 (Advanced Level), familiar with WordPerfect 5.2 and 6.0, MS Word for Windows 2.0 and Lotus 1-2-3."

3. One of Amanda Stevens' Summary of Qualifications' claims (page 148) is the following:

"Reliable, dedicated worker…"

We backed this up with:

"Worked continuously without taking breaks and without requiring supervision."

4. And Robert Miller's claim (page 145) is:

"Extremely versatile—can undertake many different job functions with ease."

We backed this up with:

"Responsible for all aspects of the department, from client assistance to petty cash to office security."

"Assumed additional job positions when necessary, e.g., handled switchboard—200 calls per day," etc.

I could go on and on. But by now I'm sure you get the idea. The point here is that anyone can form a Summary of Qualifications made up of a bunch of empty phrases or claims, but you can do better than that. You should make yours mean something. Substantiate your claims and you'll stand above all the others—because as you have seen, it's not just what you *say* you can do, it's what you *prove* you can do that makes an employer really take notice!

How to Make Yourself Look Great Even When You're Not Perfect

The clerical workers behind the sample resumes really shine with their new After versions. Your resume should make you shine, too. And don't think you have to be perfect to make a good impression. In fact, the candidates behind the resumes you have just read possess all kinds of flaws, yet they still come out looking great. Anyone can form a great resume, no matter what his or her imperfections. We all have flaws and weaknesses of one kind or another, but they don't have to keep you from looking your best.

Besides major resume problems like employment gaps and irrelevant jobs that you've already learned how to handle (in the sample resumes and Chapter 7), there are all kinds of other negatives, big and small, you can learn to beat. Again, the sample resumes are good examples for showing you how.

Here are some of the flaws of the sample resume candidates:

- Sandra completely lacks computer skills.
- Cheryl types only 35 words per minute.
- Harriet types only 40 words per minute.
- Vivian's work experience consists of only two hours per week.
- Rhonda lacks dicta and math skills.

Some of these are noticeable in the Before versions of their resumes, but not nearly as or not at all noticeable in the Afters. That's because we emphasized the positive and ignored or disguised any negatives.

Emphasize what you want to—not what you think you have to

Emphasize what is best for you and your resume, deemphasize anything that is not. All it takes is a little creativity. Camouflage, eliminate, or turn it around to work in your favor.

For instance, Cheryl and Harriet both listed low typing speeds on their Before versions; in the After versions, we didn't mention speed at all. Instead, we stressed their other typing strength—accuracy! "Typing 35 words per minute" became "accurate keyboarding abilities."

Vivian had only two hours a week of working experience, but we treated it like any regular job. We played it up with detailed job descriptions to give her full credit for her work.

Rhonda felt she lacked dicta and math skills, so we completely ignored these. Instead, we focused on her many other strong technical skills and impressive abilities. Few employers would notice anything missing after reading about all that she can do.

Sandra lacks computer skills, a real shortcoming for today's secretary, so we did the best we could with what she had. We renamed the "Technical Skills and Special Abilities" section "Special Skills and Abilities" and pulled out as many other strengths as possible.

Beat your own imperfections

Whatever your flaws are, they don't have to show up on your resume. Certainly, don't blindly stick things in because you think you have to reveal them. On the contrary, your resume should never divulge your weaknesses. When you do decide to leave things out, don't start worrying that this will immediately get noticed and put you out of the running—it won't, as long as you cleverly work around your flaws and make the most of what you *do* have.

Remember, always emphasize what is best for your resume and deemphasize, camouflage, or eliminate anything that brings you down, so that even if you're not perfect (and who is?), you can still come out looking great!

How to Modify Your Tailored Resume to Fit Any Job Position

You have learned throughout this book that tailoring is the key to your winning resume. But don't think you have to start a whole new resume from scratch for every new position you apply for. As you have seen from the double version sample resumes, once you have tailored your resume to one position, you can easily modify it to fit different jobs just by shifting things around.

Usually only minor changes are necessary. You'll need to change the Job Objective. You may have to alter your Summary of Qualifications and reorganize or shift the order of your job duties and positions to put the focus in the right place. You'll probably need to play up some jobs while scaling down others. In some cases you may need to switch from a chronological to a functional style format. But it's really not hard. Anytime you need to modify your resume for a new position, just refer to the double version sample resumes to remind you how to do it. Use them as your reference guide and you won't go wrong.

If you don't have a computer

If you don't own a computer, it's important to get access to one. Don't think you can get away without it. Word processing your resume is a must. Handwritten copies are for job hunters who want to bury themselves and typewritten ones have become extinct, for good reason. For one thing, you can't shift or alter a typewritten page. Thus, your entire resume would have to be retyped every time you make a change. Second, the look of a typewritten resume wouldn't stand much of a chance against today's high-tech competition. So if you don't currently have access to a computer and printer, get it. Here are some suggestions:

- Ask a friend or family member to let you use theirs.
- Submit a clearly typed or neatly prepared handwritten copy to a print shop or resume word processing service. Have them put it on diskette, so that anytime you need to make changes, they can produce a new copy for you at minimal cost.
- Check with your local library; some have computers available for members to use.

In Conclusion

You've analyzed sample resumes and picked up all kinds of helpful pointers along the way to help you finish up your own rough draft.

Now you're into the final inning. Chapter 9 will show you how to turn that rough draft into a finished resume, ready to go.

9

Preparing the Final Draft

It's time to turn your rough draft into final polished form. First, you will carefully review your resume to make sure you've done everything right. Then you'll polish and refine your resume and add finishing touches to put it into top shape.

This chapter will help you do all that with a comprehensive checklist and last-minute tips, including how to save resume space, how to polish and tighten your resume, how to avoid the spelling trap, and how to proofread again and again for a resume that's perfect.

First, print your resume if you haven't already done so, following the general instructions in Chapter 1 for form and layout and using the sample resumes in Chapter 8 as your guide. Carefully analyze your resume. See how it looks. Read it out loud. Listen to how it sounds.

Is it too long? Too short? Is it attractive? Does it read smoothly? Are there any mistakes? Is it properly tailored? Does it sell you the way it should?

Here's a checklist and basic review to help you make sure everything's on track.

Checklist—Did You Do It Right?

Form and style

- Did you leave a one-inch margin all around the page?
- Did you leave adequate space between sections to give your resume a clean look?

- Did you bold and capitalize all headings, job titles, and course titles?

- Did you keep to one page, or at least not go over one and a half to two pages?

- Did you use at least a 20-pound bond, preferably white, high-quality paper?

- Did you use a high-quality printer for a dark and crisp print?

- Did you form your resume in an appropriate style for your situation?

  Chronological—for a steady, relevant work history with no visible shortcomings.

  Functional—for special situations or resume problems.

- Does your resume have a flawless, professional look that demands attention?

The Job Objective

- Did you avoid vague, general job objectives?

- Did you avoid flowery and me-oriented job statements and futuristic career goals?

- Is your job objective focused, clear, and specific to the particular position you're applying for?

The Summary of Qualifications

- Did you address the four fundamental employer requirements: dependability, experience, skills, and personality?

- Did you precisely match your skills and features to the requirements of the job you're applying for and/or highlight the most outstanding things about you?

- Did you add powerful adjectives to describe yourself?

The Job History

- Did you enhance all job duties by building powerful job descriptions using the What, How, Who Phrase-Building Formula?

- Did you quantify your job duties by adding concrete numbers or percentages?

- Did you replace all plain words with professional verbs?

- Did you add people-skill provers?
- Did you add special achievements?
- Did you add any positive employer comments?
- Did you emphasize only the most relevant and important positions and job duties to the job you're applying for now, by detailing them and positioning them first?
- Did you eliminate all irrelevant positions?
- Did you camouflage any problems with job order or job dates by using a Functional Style Resume and following the special tips and advice in Chapter 7?
- Did you include job descriptions that back up the claims you made in your Summary of Qualifications?

Education and Training

- Did you properly position the Education section on your resume:
  - *After* relevant work experience in most cases.
  - *Before* work experience if you're a new grad with barely any experience or if your education is more relevant or important than any of the jobs you've held.
- Did you include all relevant courses, training, seminars, and workshops?
- Did you avoid listing course subjects and turn them into skills instead?

Technical Skills and Special Abilities

- Did you list all of your technical skills, special abilities, and best characteristic features?
- Did you make sure not to take anything for granted, to include everything you've used, learned, or know?
- Did you position the most up-to-date or popular technical skills first?

Languages and Memberships

- Did you include any foreign languages you felt would be helpful to the job you're applying for now?
- Did you avoid listing unrelated memberships or affiliations and include only relevant ones in your field?

References

- Did you avoid listing actual references on your resume and have them printed on a separate sheet instead?

Career Changers

- Did you use the functional style resume to create a relevant work experience section?

New Grads

- Did you avoid the inexperienced new grad look by positioning any relevant experience before Education?

Reentering the Workforce

- Did you use the Functional Style Resume to deemphasize job dates?

Overqualifieds

- Did you use the Functional Style to make your resume appropriate to the job you're applying for?

If you answered yes to all of these questions, then you've done a great job. If you missed anything or need to correct anything, do it now.

Last-Minute Extras

Time for the finishing touches. Before your resume goes out into the job world, you want to make sure it looks and sounds perfect. That's why now you're going to polish and tighten every phrase and paragraph, confirm you've spelled each and every word correctly, and make sure you've properly utilized every inch of space.

Tips for Saving Resume Space

Once you've printed your resume in good form, you might be dismayed to find that you didn't quite make the one-page limit. A few lines or a whole paragraph might be forcing you onto a second page. Don't give in just yet. Throughout this book, I've briefly mentioned various ways to save space or trim your resume. Here's a basic recap of what they are, and more:

1. When listing your job positions, don't include full addresses for employers or companies. There's no need to take up valuable resume space with specific street names or zip codes. It's sufficient to list cities and states only.

   For instance, instead of:

   1995-1996   **SECRETARY**

   Lighting World

   55 Carter Road, Albany NY 10002

   try:

   1995-1996   **SECRETARY,** Lighting World, Albany

   This way, you use one line instead of two or three.

2. Do the same with your Education section. Streamline each listing into one line instead of two.

   For example, instead of:

   1995-1996   **SECRETARIAL CERTIFICATE**

   Taylor's Business College

   try:

   1995-1996   **SECRETARIAL CERTIFICATE,** Taylor's Business College

3. Put your Summary of Qualifications and Technical Skills and Special Abilities sections into paragraph rather than point form. You'll gain an extra line or two, or maybe even more.

4. Bunch Languages and Memberships into your Technical Skills and Special Abilities section or omit them entirely.

5. Avoid unnecessary subheadings like "Job duties included," "Main Function," "Course requirements included," and "Program of study included." All these are space-wasters that your resume can easily do without.

6. Cut excess wording or drop verbose phrases (see Polishing and Tightening for more on this).

There are many ways to save resume space. Keep the above pointers in mind. Refer to the sample resumes to help you, and fiddle around with your resume until you get it right. Sometimes, just getting rid of a line or two will suddenly allow the whole resume to fall nicely in place on one page.

Polishing and Tightening

A tightly formed resume is what you want yours to be. Excess wording or loose phrases drag a resume down. Tight phrases have more impact. They are smooth and easy to read. Not only does a tightly formed resume fit better onto one page, it appeals to an employer because it puts all your points across quickly and powerfully.

By now, you've probably already come up with good phrases from following the instructions in Chapter 3 and analyzing the sample resumes. But sometimes, unless you're alerted to exactly what not to put in, you end up with extra words that weaken your resume's impact. So, let's weed out all the excess. Here's how. Look at this example of a loose phrase:

> "Answered <u>all the</u> incoming calls <u>of the company</u> of <u>approximately</u> 80 calls per day <u>which</u> included handling <u>the</u> clients' questions and concerns and redirecting <u>them to the</u> appropriate departments."

Although this phrase properly details the job duty, there's something wrong with the way it's constructed. It's not tight. It's too wordy. There are unnecessary words that don't make for smooth reading. The underlined words are the superfluous ones. Take them out, and you get this sleeker version:

> "Answered 80 incoming calls per day; handled client questions and concerns and redirected callers to appropriate departments."

The revised statement is so much better: It's simpler, it's tighter, and it has no unnecessary verbiage!

Don't Fall Into the Spelling Trap

Your resume's ready, you say? Wait. Don't fall into the spelling trap. As a secretary or office worker, you, more than anyone else, should have impeccable spelling skills and top-notch accuracy. Spell one word wrong on your resume and it will indicate either that you're careless or that you don't know how to spell, both real flaws for someone in your field. Unfortunately, spelling and typographical errors are common resume spoilers. Don't let your hard work go down the drain. Analyze every word to make sure it's flawless. Take the time to consult a dictionary for any words you're unsure of, or use a spell checker on your computer—it will prove to be more than worth it.

Proofreading—Review It Once, Twice, and Over Again

When you think your resume is completely ready, that's when the real proofreading can begin. Surprised? Don't be. Because that's when you'll pick up all kinds of errors you never thought you would.

Typos are the worst and can easily slip by even upon a thorough reading. Here are some tips for catching them:

- Try reading every line in your resume backwards—right to left instead of left to right.

- Recruit a second pair of eyes—have someone else, such as a friend or family member, look it over. It's amazing how an annoying little typo can get missed ten times and then suddenly be caught by someone else.

Once you've finished proofreading and you think the resume's perfect, let it sit for a day. When you come back to it, reread it once more, and if it's still fine, you'll know it's ready to go.

In Conclusion

Well, that's it. You've done it. Your resume's ready to go. But it can't go alone. It needs to be teamed up with its inseparable partner—the cover letter. I know what you're thinking, "Oh no, more work for me." Well, not exactly. Chapter 10 makes cover letter writing a snap. It practically hands you all the parts of the cover letter you'll ever need. So, for your quickest, easiest, and most effective cover letter yet, stay tuned.

10
The Cover Letter
Preparing Your Dynamite Resume Companion

You've finished your whole resume. Before you pack it up and send it out, you need a cover letter for the finishing touch. But it's not really the finishing touch at all. It's the first thing the employer will see. Before the employer lays eyes on any part of the resume you so diligently toiled away at, he or she will gain the very first impression of you from your cover letter. So it's important to take the time to make it perfect.

A good cover letter contains a delicate balance of information. It should be direct and to the point without being too sketchy or sounding dry. It should grab attention with impressive things about you without revealing too much from your resume or sounding repetitious. Most of all, it must be flawlessly written with perfect spelling, grammar, punctuation, and sentence structure. Sound like a tall order for one small letter? Don't worry. You can easily tackle it with the instructions in this chapter.

First, you'll learn about problem cover letters and how to avoid them; then you'll learn the fundamentals of cover letter writing, and how to form the cover letter parts. You'll view powerful sample cover letters, and best of all, you'll choose exact, ready-made phrases to make forming your own cover letter a breeze. Read on, pay attention, and together, we'll make it dynamite!

Problem Cover Letters and How to Avoid Them

The cover letter serves as an introduction or cover sheet to your resume and basically states the fact that you're sending your resume and why. A clear, simple letter is basically all you need, especially when you already have a powerful resume. Often people do too much to their cover letters and end up with the following problems.

Too much cover letter

Yes, a cover letter is the first thing an employer sees, and yes, it's important to make a great first impression, but don't go overboard. Don't put too much in your cover letter.

Avoiding life stories. One type of "too much cover letter" is the one that includes your whole life story. Take this example:

> I am currently a student at Humberwood University and I will receive my B.A. in November. I am an honor student majoring in economics and minoring in mathematics. I still have two courses to take and once I finish those, which I believe will be the end of April, I will be available to work for you. I am also enrolled in three different computer training programs. I plan to finish two of these in April, and although I'll still have one more course left, I will be free to take on full-time employment as this course meets only one night a week.

Never go rambling on in the cover letter about everything you did or are planning to do. Employers don't want to hear it, nor do they have the time or patience to read it. Besides, you surely wouldn't want an employer to plow through something that makes you appear so unfocused and disorganized.

Avoiding repetitious detail. Others put too much in their cover letters by repeating duties and skills from their resumes. Take a look at this example:

I have worked as a receptionist and I have booked appointments, filed, input computer data, answered phones, and am familiar with bookkeeping, mathematics, Macintosh and IBM computers, DOS, Word for Windows, WordPerfect, Microsoft Word, am fluent in Spanish...

Never put details of your resume in the cover letter. You will learn how to summarize yourself and emphasize certain key points about yourself, but that's all. There's no need to reiterate each and every duty or skill in the cover letter.

Too little cover letter

On the other hand, some cover letters have the opposite problem. Don't just say, "Here's my resume" and nothing else. Take this example:

I am submitting my resume for your consideration. I have a lot of secretarial experience and would like to work for your company. I look forward to hearing from you soon.

Short, dry, and boring doesn't make a good cover letter either. It's important to find the right balance of information, as this is one of the keys to making your cover letter ideal.

The Ideal Cover Letter—Clear and Simple Plus Attention-Getting Appeal

Your cover letter should be clear, simple, and to the point. It should read like a professional business letter yet should possess a combination of enthusiasm and attention-getting appeal.

Before we delve into the contents of the cover letter and learn how to form its parts, let's first become familiar with its fundamentals—its all-important layout and appearance and the general rules for writing it.

Basic Cover Letter Format—Fundamentals You Need to Get Started

Look at the basic cover letter format (Fig. 10-1 on page 183).

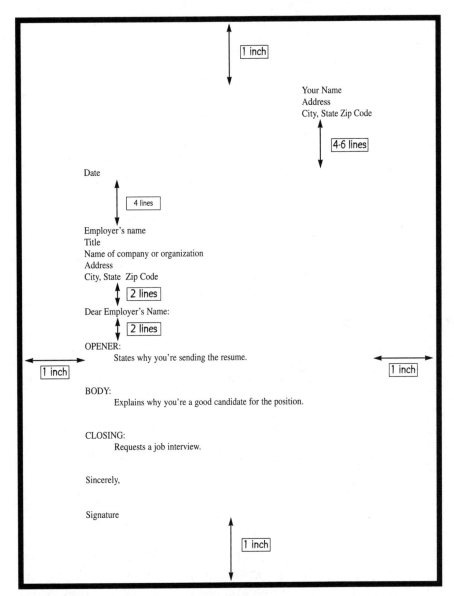

Figure 10-1. Basic cover letter format.

Notice that the cover letter follows the basic layout of a standard business letter. These are the general guidelines to follow:

- Leave at least a one-inch (2.5 cm) margin all around the page (left, right, top, and bottom). You can even justify the right margin for a nicer effect.

- Place your name and address (or letterhead information) at the top right or left of your letter. If you wish, you can center it and even bold or italicize it to give it a real letterhead look.

- Leave four to six lines between your letterhead information and the date and another four lines between the date and the employer or addressee information.

- Make sure your addressee information is complete with employer's name, title, company name, address, city, state, and zip code.
- Always try to address your cover letter to a specific person. Call the company or organization to get the employer or hiring manager's name. If you're responding to a blind ad or for any reason can't obtain a specific name, then write "Dear Human Resources Manager" or "Dear Hiring Manager"—both are better than the old "To Whom It May Concern."
- Keep your cover letter short, one page with no more than three to five paragaphs.

The Cover Letter Parts

The cover letter consists of three basic parts with each one designed to say something specific and make a certain point.
These three parts are:

1. The opener—which states why you're sending the resume.
2. The body—which explains why you're a good candidate for the position.
3. The closing—which requests a job interview.

The opener

The opener forms the first sentence or paragraph of your cover letter and simply states the fact that you're sending your resume and why. The opener will vary depending on your situation. An opener can be:

- in response to a newspaper ad.
- a follow-up to a friend's or contact's suggestion or recommendation.
- a follow-up to a prospective employer's request to send your resume.
- a general inquiry into a possible job opening.

Make sure to form an appropriate opener for your situation. For instance, if you are responding to a newspaper ad, an example opener for you might be:

> In response to your advertisement for a Secretary in the May 16, 1996 edition of the Denver Post, I am sending you my resume...

Always include the exact position title advertised and the name and date of the newspaper in which the ad appeared, so that the employer can instantly identify the position you are applying for.

If you're following up on a friend's or contact's suggestion or recommendation, an opener for you might read as:

> Sharon Davidson suggested that I contact you regarding the office clerk job opening in your department...

If you are following up on a prospective employer's request to send your resume, your opener might look like this:

> As per our phone conversation of December 3, 1996 regarding the administrative assistant position, I am sending you my resume as you requested.

And if you are making a general inquiry into the availability of a job (sometimes it's worth a shot), your opener can read:

> I am interested in securing employment with your company and am sending my resume for your consideration.

For a complete list of sample opener phrases to choose from, see "The Sample Phrases—Your Invaluable Cover Letter Writing Tool," coming up.

The body

The body is the crux of your cover letter. It's where you convince an employer to read on to your resume by showing that you're a good candidate for the position. This part is a bit tricky because there is no single right way to do this or exact instruction to follow. The best way to learn how to create this part of the letter is simply to view the sample cover letters and sample phrases for ideas and inspiration. Nevertheless, to help you demystify the process and organize your thoughts, the following are some basic approaches you can take.

1. Introduce yourself. First of all, be sure to briefly summarize who you are, what type of relevant positions you've held, and for how long. For example, you might say:

> I am an executive secretary with over six years of experience.

2. State what you have done or can do. Next, heighten an employer's interest in you by stating what you have done or can do. One way to do this is to provide a simple but effective summary of your duties or skills. For example:

> I can effectively handle administrative duties and am thoroughly familiar with all aspects of an office.

or:

> I am up to date and thoroughly familiar with many popular word processing programs.

Another approach you might try is to scour your resume for an impressive special point about yourself such as a special achievement, outstanding skill, or appealing personality trait—one that you feel will especially grab an employer's attention. Use this to pack extra punch in the body of your letter. For instance:

> I am a goal-oriented individual who works tirelessly to please customers and actively pulls in business with a pleasant disposition and friendly smile.

3. Link yourself to the position. Last, round off the body of your letter by including a statement that links yourself to the job you're applying for. For instance, you can say:

> I am confident that my professional training, extensive secretarial experience, and advanced computer skills would make me a valuable asset to your team.

Don't forget to address the employer's needs

As always, keep in mind the tailoring aspect and give the body of your cover letter an "I'm-talking-directly-to-the-employer" feel by making sure that anything you choose to say about yourself addresses the needs of the particular employer. For instance, if an ad emphasizes a certain requirement of a job, make sure your summary or special point about yourself relates to it directly.

Watch out for redundancy

At the same time, make sure your cover letter doesn't make your resume sound repetitious. Here are some ways to prevent this:

1. Reword. Be careful when borrowing juicy bits and chunks from your resume. You certainly don't want your cover letter to end up sounding like a duplicate of your resume, so never copy anything verbatim. Always reword phrases taken from the resume, or if you can, think of some new or different special point about you that isn't already in the resume.

2. Summarize. In the cover letter, always summarize anything detailed in the resume. You'll avoid a repetitious feel but still get to address some of the same important points.

The closing

The closing finishes off the letter by requesting a job interview and thanking the employer. Your closing might read like the following:

> I would greatly appreciate the opportunity of an interview. Please call me anytime at (123) 555-4105. Thank you for your consideration. I look forward to hearing from you.

If you prefer a more assertive approach, and you should when job hunting, instead of waiting by the phone for an employer to call, take control. Initiate the call to set up the interview. You can say:

> I will call you next week to arrange a mutually convenient time for us to meet.

Making It Error Free

The best cover letter instruction in the world will do nothing for you if your cover letter is deficient in the English department. In fact, any type of writing error will make your cover letter work against you rather than for you. Therefore, as with the resume, you must be extremely careful to make spelling, grammar, punctuation, and sentence structure flawless.

To assist you with this crucial element, the sample cover letter phrases presented can help you form an error-free cover letter instantly. Or, if you're forming your own cover letter or even parts of your own, and you're not fully confident about your writing skills, it's a good idea to have a second pair of eyes look it over (preferably someone with excellent writing abilities) to catch any spelling, grammatical, or typographical errors.

The Sample Phrases—Your Invaluable Cover Letter Writing Tool

Time to start your cover letter. The following is a great guide for you. It contains a large selection of exact sample phrases you can mix and match. Choose the ones you like best, that sound the most like you, or that say what you most want to say. Pick an opener, a body (the body will require extra forming on your part), and a closing. Just replace the underlined words, and voilà, they become your own. Add or change anything to fit your own situation, fill in any gaps, and you'll have a dynamite cover letter ready to go!

Don't forget to take a peek at the sample cover letters at the end of this chapter for more ideas, and to see how the all the cover letter parts look once they're placed together in their final form.

Sample opener phrases

Here are sample openers for four different situations.

1. Responding to a newspaper ad

In response to your advertisement for the Secretary/ Receptionist position in the July 15, 1996 edition of the Los Angeles Times, I am sending you my resume.

This letter is in regard to your legal secretarial job opening as advertised in the June 30, 1996 issue of the New York Times. Enclosed please find my resume, which details my related work experience and education.

Extra dynamic openers:

I read your advertisement for an administrative assistant in last Saturday's Boston Globe with great enthusiasm, as I have the exact qualifications you are looking for and have been searching for a position such as this one.

I was excited to see your ad for an Executive Secretary that appeared in this week's Washington Post, as I believe I am a perfect match for the position. Enclosed is my resume for your review.

2. Following up on a friend's or contact's suggestion or recommendation

Roberta Gardens suggested I contact you regarding the possible job opening in your department for a data entry clerk.

I spoke with <u>Marianne Walker last week</u> and <u>she</u> mentioned that you are currently looking for an <u>executive secretary</u>.

<u>Brian Braun</u>, who works in <u>your Payroll Department</u>, suggested that I contact you regarding the <u>Accounting Clerk</u> job opening.

<u>Bob Williams</u> spoke to you <u>the other day</u> about my possible candidacy for a <u>supervisory office position</u> within your company. Thank you for considering me for the position.

Extra dynamic opener:

<u>Loretta Swanson</u>, a <u>senior secretary</u> in your <u>firm</u>, informed me that you were looking for a <u>mature, experienced individual</u> to handle the administrative duties of <u>two junior attorneys</u>. I believe I am that person and can positively contribute to your team.

3. Following up on an employer's request to send your resume

As per our telephone conversation of <u>October 28, 1996</u> regarding the <u>Administrative Assistant</u> position, I am sending you my resume.

Thank you for taking the time to discuss with me your company's job opening for a <u>bookkeeper</u> and my potential candidacy. As you requested, I am sending you my resume.

In response to our discussion <u>this morning</u> about the job opening in your <u>word processing department</u>, I am sending you my resume.

4. Making a general inquiry

I wish to secure employment as a <u>Data Entry Operator</u> with your <u>organization</u> and am submitting my resume for your consideration.

I am interested in acquiring a position as a <u>secretary/receptionist</u> in your <u>company</u>.

I am extremely interested in obtaining a <u>legal secretarial</u> position with your <u>firm</u>.

Extra dynamic opener:

Would your company be interested in hiring a highly motivated <u>certified professional secretary</u>?

Sample body phrases

Because the body is the personalized part of your cover letter, use these phrases for ideas and inspiration rather than copying them directly. If you wish, lift certain phrases right off and mix and match parts of them with your own until you get a body that's just right for you and the particular job you're applying for.

Remember, when forming the body of your letter, always address the needs of the particular employer but never repeat things verbatim from your resume—summarize or reword instead!

I have four years' experience in the clerical field, can handle all aspects of an office, and am thoroughly familiar with several popular word processing programs. I believe that my combined education, work experience, and technical skills would make me a valuable addition to your organization.

I can bring enthusiasm, commitment, and a high level of professionalism to your company. I have six years' experience as an office assistant in a property management company where I have acquired strong interpersonal skills, top-notch priority-setting abilities, and a keen business sense. I am confident that I can be a valuable asset to your company and make a significant contribution to your team.

As you will see from my resume, I am a dedicated, results-driven secretary with eight years of experience who doesn't mind working hard to get a job done right! In my previous position, I often worked overtime with my manager to meet emergency deadlines for special research projects. I am confident that my high level of dedication coupled with my professional experience and technical skills will make me a valuable asset to your office.

My ten years of experience as an Administrative Assistant for the general manager of Benson's Hotels and Resorts have prepared me for the type of position you need to fill. I possess exceptional customer relations skills, can handle multiple administrative duties and general office tasks, and possess expert bookkeeping abilities. In addition, I am thoroughly familiar with every aspect of the hotel industry and possess a wide range of technical and computer skills.

I believe you will find my background well suited to your position. As you will note from my enclosed resume, I am an extremely hardworking medical secretary with two years of hospital experience. I thrive in high-pressure situations, have fostered an excellent rapport with all patients and hospital staff, and am familiar with several word processing packages.

Sample closing phrases

I would greatly appreciate the opportunity of an interview. Please contact me any time at my home number at (123) 555-4772. Thank you for your consideration. I look forward to hearing from you.

I would be most interested in meeting with you to discuss how my qualifications can further complement your needs. May I take the liberty of contacting you to set up an interview? I will call your office next week to arrange a mutually convenient time.

I am eager to personally discuss my qualifications with you and how I can further contribute to your organization. Please call me at (123) 555-3696. Thank you for your time and consideration. I look forward to speaking with you.

For a general inquiry:

Should a position become available, please contact me at your earliest convenience.

Should such a position become available, I would appreciate your considering my application.

Though there may be no job vacancies at this time, I think it would be worthwhile for us to meet to discuss my possible candidacy and how I might be able to contribute to your organization in the future.

Five Sample Cover Letters—How All the Parts Come Together

Time to put together all the parts you've chosen and formed. The assortment of sample cover letters on the following pages can help you. Analyze them to see how the opener, body, and closing work together to form powerful, effective letters.

Rhonda Rice
11 Salinger Court
Dallas, TX 10002

September 28, 1996

Hiring Manager
Solway Marketing Inc.
4550 Sheridan Blvd.
Dallas, TX 10002

Dear Hiring Manager:

In response to your advertisement for a Secretary/Receptionist position as advertised in the September 28, 1996, edition of the Dallas Morning News, I am sending you my resume.

As a secretary who has worked for the head office of a leading wine store chain, I have gained the experience and skills necessary to handle a wide variety of responsibilities. I am a motivated, fast worker with excellent computer skills and am confident that I can meet the demands of your position.

I would very much appreciate the opportunity of an interview. I will take the liberty of calling your office next week to arrange a mutually convenient time.

Thank you for your kind consideration of my application.

Sincerely yours,

Rhonda Rice

See Rhonda Rice's corresponding resume (page 113).

November 23, 1995

Mr. Nick Brunell, Manager
Shaw's Cable Company
970 3rd Street
Denver, CO 10002

Dear Mr. Brunell:

I am interested in acquiring a position as a Customer Service Representative in your company and am sending you my resume for your consideration.

As you will see from my resume, I am a hardworking, versatile individual with several years of experience in client services and related office positions. I possess excellent oral communication skills, good problem-solving abilities, knowledge of computer programs, and am mechanically inclined.

I believe that my experience and skills, combined with my ability to establish an excellent rapport with clients/customers, would make me a valuable asset to your company. I would be most interested in meeting with you to discuss how my qualifications can complement your needs. I can be reached at my home number (123) 555-6244. Thank you for your time. I look forward to speaking with you.

Sincerely,

Robert Miller

See Robert Miller's corresponding resume (page 145).

Vivian Clark
278 Orchard Park Road
Phoenix, AZ 10002

November 6, 1996

Director
Department of Human Resources
Desert Falls Hospital
8112 Sun Drive
Phoenix, AZ 10002

Dear Human Resources Director:

Enclosed please find a copy of my resume in response to your medical secretarial job opening as advertised in the Phoenix Gazette on November 4, 1996.

I have successfully completed a two-year office administration program with honors and am presently working as a medical secretary. I have gained good organizational and communication skills and have learned how to effectively handle all aspects of a medical office. I possess good technical skills and excellent knowledge of many word processing programs.

I am confident that my training and work experience, combined with my ability and eagerness to learn, would make me a valuable asset to your department. Please refer to my resume for a detailed look at my background.

I would very much appreciate the opportunity of an interview. Please contact me at home (123) 555-7248 or at work (123) 555-4310. Thank your for your kind consideration of my application. I look forward to hearing from you soon.

Sincerely yours,

Vivian Clark

See Vivian Clark's corresponding resume (page 157)

Suzy Galloway
46 Plumwood Drive
Philadelphia, PA 10002

June 21, 1996

Ms. Janice Forest-Black, President
Just Right Secretarial and Printing Services
1622 Horton Street
Philadelphia, PA 10002

Dear Ms. Forest-Black:

I read your advertisement for a personal office assistant and word processor in the Saturday edition of the Philadelphia Daily News with great enthusiasm. I possess all the qualifications you indicated and believe I am a perfect match for the position.

As you will see from my enclosed resume, I have fast, accurate keyboarding abilities (110 w.p.m.) acquired from many years of working as a Dicta Typist and Senior Secretary. No job is too big and no deadline too tight. I am also a meticulous proofreader with superior writing and editing abilities, and have excellent references attached.

I am eager to personally discuss my qualifications with you, and would greatly appreciate the opportunity of an interview. I will call your office next week to set up a mutually convenient time for us to meet. I look forward to speaking with you.

Sincerely,

Suzy Galloway

Extra dynamic cover letter.

Alisa Young
371 Barton Avenue
Pittsburgh, PA 10002

December 4, 1996

Mr. Jeffrey Woodruff, President
Kingsway Plastics
44 Hill Street West
Unit 2500
Pittsburgh, PA 10002

Dear Mr. Woodruff:

Don Wood, an assistant manager in your company, recently informed me about a job opening for an Executive Secretary and suggested that I send you my resume.

I am an Executive Secretary with four years' experience working for the Vice President of a plastics manufacturer. I can bring to your organization the highest level of professionalism and top-notch priority-setting abilities. I possess excellent computer skills and am thoroughly familiar with every popular word processing program. As well, I am an extremely organized individual with highly developed written language skills.

May I take the liberty of contacting you to set up an interview? I will call your office next week to see if we can arrange a mutually convenient time.

Thank you for your consideration of my application.

Sincerely yours,

Alisa Young

Cover Letter Do's and Don'ts

By now you probably already have one great cover letter draft. Before you finalize it, however, note the following do's and don'ts:

1. Don't ever handwrite your cover letter as some job hunters think is acceptable—it's not. Always print it in a font that complements your resume and use the same color and quality paper as your resume.

2. Don't mention salary—ever! (This applies even if an ad asks you to include it.) You might place yourself out of the running if you state a figure that's too high or you could look underqualified or lose out if you provide a number that's too low.

3. Above all, don't use the cover letter to explain negatives about yourself. Never try to explain why you've been fired or laid off or lack steady employment, skills, or experience. For example, if you start your cover letter with, "Even though I have no experience..." or "The reason my jobs were so short is because...," you'll have just shot down everything you've worked so hard to deemphasize in your resume, and you'll turn off all employers instantly.

One note of caution, though: Do be prepared to tactfully explain any negatives about yourself or your job situation in the job interview. That's where these things might come up, if they come up at all.

Checklist—Did You Do It Right?

Once you've formed your final cover letter draft, use this checklist and basic review to help make sure everything's on track.

- Did you set up your cover letter with adequate margins (at least one inch all around) and spacing and include no more than three to five paragraphs?

- Does your opener clearly introduce the fact that you're sending your resume and why?

- Does your body convincingly explain why you're a good candidate for the position:

  - by introducing yourself

  - and stating what you have done or can do?

- Did you address specific needs or requirements of the job you're applying for?

- Did you avoid repeating details from your resume (and re-word or summarize things instead)?

- Does your closing thank the employer and request a job interview?

In Conclusion

That's it. Now you're done. You have a fabulous resume and a great cover letter to go with it. What do you do with them? Read on to find out how to get it safely where you want it to go.

11

Simply Divine and Ready to Go

What to Do with Your Resume Package

It's time to send off your resume and cover letter package on its job-getting mission. There are two ways to do this: by fax or by mail. Here are tips to get your resume to its destination in the best possible shape.

Faxing Your Resume

Today, many job ads require you to fax your resume. It's important to fax it when an ad tells you to do so. Faxing is a modern method that gets your resume to an employer fast—a method that employers have come to expect. There's no sense in mailing yours and losing a job opportunity to the hundreds of applicants who had theirs arrive on the employer's desk a week before.

The trouble with faxes is an aesthetic one. Anyone who's been on the receiving end of a fax knows that what comes out isn't quite like what went in. Thus, you may be concerned that some of your hard work will go unnoticed. For instance, your nice paper quality becomes irrelevant when faxed, and even your font selections or nice resume layout can be affected as, at times, words or sections can become altered or smudged-looking as they go through the fax.

Though it's hard to control what happens to your resume and cover letter during its travels by fax, there are things you can do to help it along. Here are some suggestions.

Follow up by mail

If the ad provides a mailing address as well as a fax number (or if you can obtain a mailing address), you can always follow up your fax with a mailed copy of your resume.

In addition to ensuring that an employer sees your resume in its best form, the mailing can also give you a second chance to get an employer to notice you. By fax, your resume will arrive with dozens or even hundreds of others in the first few days following the placement of an ad. Yours can easily get overlooked in the deluge of paper. A mailed follow-up resume, however, demands extra attention. There is a drawback, though: Companies or employers may be irritated by the double paper attempt. But it's more likely that they may not even realize it's a second copy and just reconsider you.

Faxing it right

Remember always to fax your resume with your accompanying cover letter (faxing doesn't mean you can leave the cover letter out). Include a fax cover sheet or, better yet, affix a Post-it fax note right onto the top corner of your cover letter, routing it to the proper person in the proper department. Always double-check the fax number to make sure you've got the right place.

Mailing Your Resume

When mailing your resume as an original response to an ad or as a follow-up to a fax, take proper care to do it right.

Keep it pressed and clean

Keep your sheets neat and crisp. Make sure they don't look crumpled or worn as if many people have handled them.

Send it in style

Use a 9 × 12 inch white envelope. A large envelope allows you to send your resume without folding it so that it arrives looking as professional as when you took it out of the printer.

A white envelope is nicer than a manila one; it has a professional business look that stands out from the others.

Making Sure It Arrived

Get into the habit of following things up with a phone call. You've worked too hard to just sit back and "guess" that it got there okay. Whether you've sent it by mail or fax, treat your resume with the importance it deserves. Follow up with a phone call to make sure it arrived.

By doing this, not only are you saying "I'm important" and demanding extra attention, but you can also use the opportunity to try to set up an interview, especially if your cover letter is the take-charge kind that specified you would be the one to call and set it up.

Making the Call—Professional and Businesslike Always

Carry your professional image from your resume right through to the way you handle yourself on the phone. Always be polite, friendly, and businesslike to everyone you come into contact with, no matter whom you're speaking to, whether you think it's someone important or not. Don't think, "Oh, it's just the receptionist." He or she might be a prospective coworker, or might have even been given the job of screening phone applicants.

Preparing to Receive an Employer's Call

If you're waiting for an employer to call *you*, do make sure you can be reached at the phone number listed on your resume and cover letter. If you won't be home, make sure there's someone or something (like an answering machine) to take the call for you.

Don't leave just any message on your machine. The worst are those cute little messages with your five-year-old talking, accompanied by Disney music in the background. Okay, it is your home and not an office, but remember, you are expecting a business call and you should be properly prepared for it. Here's a good tip: If you have to leave on an answering machine, record a specific message for employers and you'll come off looking like a real pro!

In Conclusion

That's all it takes. Fax it, mail it, follow it up with a phone call, and you've properly sent your resume and cover letter off into the job world.

Conclusion

Updating Your Resume—Now and in the Future

So, you did it. Congratulations! Break out the bubbly and celebrate. You've worked hard to make your resume the best it can be. Now you have a truly terrific presentation of yourself.

But it doesn't stop here. Resume writing is a continuous process. Just as you haven't stopped living, working, and learning, so your resume should never stand still. It should grow and change as you do. It needs to reflect all your new professional and academic achievements along the way.

Every time you acquire a new skill, gain new knowledge in your field, take a new course, become a member of an organization, start or finish another job, or do anything that further contributes to your job goal—add it to your resume.

And don't ever forget your crucially important role in the office world. Make sure that your resume always represents you powerfully and professionally.

Good luck in your job search, and may your new resume, and resumes ahead, win you the best jobs and a bright working future!

Appendix

Your Guide to Professional Associations

Here's a guide to professional secretarial and related associations around the world.

In the United States

Professional Secretaries International (PSI)
10502 NW Ambassador Drive
P.O. Box 20404
Kansas City, MO 64195-0404
Tel: (816) 891-6600
Fax: (816) 891-9118
    Professional Secretaries International (PSI) is the leading organization for secretaries with over 40,000 members and 700 chapters around the world.

National Association of Executive Secretaries (NAES)
900 S. Washington Street, No. G-13
Falls Church, VA 22046
Tel: (703) 237-8616

National Association of Legal Secretaries International (NALS)
2448 East 81st Street, Ste. 3400
Tulsa, OK 74137
Tel: (918) 493-3540
Fax: (918) 493-5784

American Association for Medical Assistants
20 North Wacker Drive, Ste. 1575
Chicago, IL 60606
Tel: (312) 899-1500
or: 1-800-228-2262

**Professional Association of Health Care
Office Managers**
461 East 10 Mile Road
Pensacola, FL 32534
Tel: (904) 474-9460
or: 1-800-451-9311

American Association for Medical Transcription
P.O. Box 576187
Modesto, CA 95357-6187
Tel: (209) 551-0883
or: 1-800-982-2182

**National Association of Educational Office
Professionals (NAEOP)**
P.O. Box 12619
Wichita, KS 67277
Tel: (316) 942-4822
Fax: (316) 942-7100

Executive Women International (EWI)
515 South 700 East, Ste. 2E
Salt Lake City, UT 84102
Tel: (801) 355-2800

9 to 5 National Association of Working Women
238 West Wisconsin Avenue, Ste. 700
Milwaukee, WI 53203

In Canada

Association of Administrative Assistants
P.O. Box 5107, Station A
Toronto, Ontario M5W 1N4
Tel: (416) 638-0827

Ontario Medical Secretaries Association
525 University Avenue, Ste. 300
Toronto, Ontario M5G 2K7
Tel: (416) 599-2580

International

European Association of Professional Secretaries
Hoje Gladsaxe 43 7tv
DK-2860 Soeborg, Denmark
Tel: 44980115
Fax: 39667656

Institute of Qualified Private Secretaries
46 Kittiwake Drive
Kidderminster, Worc, UK 10 4RS
Tel: (01562) 822593

Inter-American Federation of Secretaries (FIAS)
Apartado Postal (01)78
San Salvador, El Salvador
Tel: 232561
Fax: 235446

Institute of Professional Secretaries
G.P.O. Box 2950 DD
Melbourne, Vic. 3001, Australia

International Federation of Shorthand and Typewriting
Postfach 12 02 69
53044 Bonn, Germany
Tel: 228 251509

Deutscher Sekretarinnen-Verband (DSV)
Geschaftsstelle
Nietzschestrasse 89
67063 Ludwigshafen, Germany
Tel: 621 695965
Fax: 621 632158

National Secretaries' Association
P.O. Box 1241
Port of Spain, Trinidad and Tobago

Women Secretaries' Association of Thailand
6/2 Pichai Rd.
Dusit
Bangkok 10300, Thailand
Tel: 2 2415555
Fax: 2 2430898

Index

Abilities, special, 66-69
Accounting clerk, before and after sample resume for, 136-141
Accounts receivable clerk, before and after sample resume for, 132-134
Achievements, special, 42-45, 49
Adjectives, for describing skills, 21-22
Administrative Assistant, before and after sample resumes for, 126-128, 129-131
Adverbs, for describing characteristic features, 72
American Association for Medical Assistants, 203
American Association for Medical Transcription, 204
Answering machine, to take employer calls, 201
Answering phones, sample job description for, 36
Association of Administrative Assistants, 204

Booking appointments, sample job description for, 37
Bookkeeper, before and after sample resume for, 152-154
Business school, 52-54, 57

Career changers
    before and after sample resume for, 158-160
    problems, facing, 92-93
    resume solutions for, 93-97
Career goals, see Job objectives
Certified professional secretary, 57
Characteristic features, 69-72
Checklists
    for cover letter preparation, 197-198
    for resume preparation, 173-176
Chronological style resume, 9
    format for, 6
    samples of, 113-114, 117, 120, 124-125, 128, 131, 145, 148, 157, 165
Classified ads, see Want ads
Clerical duties, see Job duties

Clerical duties, digging up, for career changers, 94-96
College graduates, see New grads
Community college, 52-54, 57
Computer knowledge, importance to job search, 97, 102-103
Computer software programs, 63
Computers, using, to create resume, 8, 172
Course curriculum, using, as skills, 57-58, 67-68, 99, 155-157
Courses, 52-55, 57
Cover letters, 180-198
    avoiding problem, 181-182
    checklist, for preparation of, 197-198
    do's and don'ts, 197
    format for, 182-184
    making error free, 187
    parts of, 184-187
    purpose of, 180, 181, 182
    sample phrases for, 188-191
    samples of, 191-196
Custom tailoring resume, see Tailoring
Customer service clerk, before and after sample resume for, 136-139
Customer service representative, before and after sample resume for, 142-145

Data entry operator, before and after sample resume for, 146-148
Data processor, before and after sample resume for, 149-151
Dates of employment, 28-29
    problems with, 106-109
Deutscher Sekretarinnen-Verband (DSV), 205

Education and training, 52-58
    forming, on resume, 57
    importance to resume, 52
    placement in resume, 55-56
    what to include, 53-55
Employer comments, to enhance job history, 45
Employer information, 30
Employers' needs, matching skills to, 20-25

Employment gaps, 106-107
Employment History, *see* Job History
Entering computer data, sample job description for, 39
Envelope, for mailing resume, 200
European Association of Professional Secretaries, 205
Executive secretary, before and after sample resume for, 126-128
Executive Women International (EWI), 204
Experience, lacking, *see* Career changers; New grads

Filing, sample job description for, 37
Filling out forms, sample job description for, 39-40
Final draft, preparing, 173-179
Financial clerk, before and after sample resume for, 161-162
Flaws, overcoming, in resume 170-171
Functional style resume, 88-92
    format for, 89
    samples of, 134, 135, 138-139, 140-141, 151, 154, 160, 162, 166
    see also Problems, conquering in resume

Handling bookkeeping, sample job description for, 39
Headings, in resume, 6-7, 8
High school, 55
Hobbies and interests, 81

Image, enhancing, 1-3, 32-48
Imperfections, beating, 170-171
Institute of Professional Secretaries, 205
Institute of Qualified Private Secretaries, 205
Inter-American Federation of Secretaries (FIAS), 205
International Federation of Shorthand and Typewriting, 205
Irrelevant jobs, 104-105

Job contacts and leads, 26
Job dates, 28-29
    problems with, 106-109
    streamlining, 108
Job descriptions, *see* Job duties
Job duties, 32-45
    adding human touch to, 41-42
    enhancing simple, 40-41
    forming descriptions for, 33-40
    organizing, 48-49
    powerful verbs for, 45-48
    special achievements, 42-45
Job history, 27-51
    dates of employment, 28-29
    job duties, 32-45
    job titles, 29-30

    main function, 30-32
Job hopper, 107-109
Job objectives, 11-16
    avoiding problem, 12-15
    vs. career goals, 14-15
    specific, 13, 14, 15-16
Job positions, organizing, 50-51
    irrelevant, 104-105
Job resources, utilizing, 26
Job retrainers, 56
Jobs, irrelevant, 104-105
Jobs, temporary, 107-108
Jobs, short term, 107-109
Job titles, 29-30

Keyboarding, *see* Typing

Languages, 68, 76-78
Legal secretary, before and after sample resumes for, 118-120, 121-125
Letters of recommendation, 84-86

Main function, of job, 30-32
Medical secretary, before and after sample resumes for, 115-117, 155-157
Memberships, 78-80
Minute taking, sample job description for, 38

9 to 5 National Association of Working Women, 204
Name, address and phone number, in resume, 10-11
National Association of Educational Office Professionals (NAEOP), 204
National Association of Executive Secretaries (NAES), 203
National Association of Legal Secretaries International (NALS), 203
National Secretaries Association, 205
New grads, 97-101
    before and after sample resume for, 155-157
    with no working experience, 99-101
    with relevant working experience, 98-99
    with unrelated working experience, 99-101
    see also Education and Training
Newspaper ads, *see* Want ads

Objective, *see* Job Objectives
Office administration courses, 52-54, 57
Office automation, 1, 62-64
Office clerk, before and after sample resumes for, 132-135, 163-165
Office machines and equipment, 63-64
Office manager, before and after sample resume for, 163-166
Office worker, value in the workplace, 1-2

Ontario Medical Secretaries Association, 204
Ordering supplies, sample job description for, 38
Outdated information
    hobbies and interests, 81
    personal data, 80-81
Overqualified individuals, 103-104
    before and after sample resume for, 163-165

Paper, for resume, 7
People skill provers, 41-42
Personal data, 80-81
Personality strengths, 69-72
Phrase-building formula, using
    to build job descriptions, 34-40
    to find special achievements, 42-45
    to spice up simplest tasks, 40-41
Phrases, sample
    for cover letters, 188-191
    for job descriptions, 35-45
Planning conventions, sample job description for, 38
Position titles, 29-30
Positive employer comments, 45
Printers, using, to create resume, 7, 8, 172
Problems, conquering in resume, 87-109
    career changers, 92-97
    employment gaps, 106-107
    irrelevant jobs, 104-105
    new grads, 97-101
    overqualifieds, 103-104
    reentering workforce, 101-103
    short-term jobs, 107-109
Professional Association of Health Care Office Managers, 204
Professional associations, 78-80
    international list of, 203-205
Professional development, 57, 74
Professional job language, replacing plain words with, 45-48
Professional Secretaries International (PSI), 57, 79, 203

Receiving visitors, job description for, 37-38
Receptionist, before and after sample resume for, 158-160
Reentering the workforce, individuals
    before and after sample resume for, 161-162
    problems, facing, 101-102
    resume solutions for, 102-103
Reference letters, 84-86
References, 82-86
Resumes
    appearance of, 5-8
    basic format for, 6
    before and after samples of, 110-166
    checklist, for preparation of, 173-176
    chronological, see Chronological style resume
    faxing, 199-200

final draft, preparing, 173-179
functional, see Functional style resume
gaining immediate attention with, 10-25
length of, 8-9, 176-177
mailing, 200
makings of, 4-5
margins, spacing, and structure of, 7-8
modifying tailored, 171-172
paper for, 7
parts of, 5, 6
polishing and tightening, 178
proofreading, 179
spelling, checking accuracy of, 178-179
tailoring, to specific job positions, see Tailoring
updating, 202

Salary, omitting, from cover letter, 197
Secretarial associations, see Professional associations
Secretarial courses, 52-54, 57
Secretarial school, 52-54, 57
Secretary
    before and after sample resume for, 112-114
    value in the workplace, 1-2
Secretary/office clerk, before and after sample resume for, 132-135
Short-term jobs, 107-109
Skills, 62-75
    characteristic features, 69-72
    discovering, 62-72
    keeping up with latest, 74-75
    lacking, 22, 102, 170-171
    matching, to employer's needs, see Summary of Qualifications
    organization of, 72-74
    special abilities, 66-69
    technical, 62-66
    underestimation of, 59-62
Software programs, 63
Space, saving, on resume, 176-177
Special abilities, 66-69
    acquired on the job, 68
    learned in college, 67-68
    natural talents, 67
Special achievements, 42-45
    organizing, 49
Special situations, see Problems, conquering, in resume
Specialized knowledge, see Special abilities
Spelling, checking accuracy of, 178-179
Summary of Qualifications, 16-26
    for career changers, 96
    do's and don'ts, 25
    forming, 17-20
    forming tailored, 20-25
    hooking employers with, 16-17
    matching, to employers needs, 20-25
    for new grads, 22-23, 99, 100-101
    proving claims made in, 25, 167-170

Tailoring
  advantages of, 14, 167
  job duties, 48-49
  job positions, 50-51
  and modifying, 25, 171-172
  Summary of Qualifications, 20-25
  whole resume, 167
Technical skills, discovering, 62-66
  computer software programs, 63
  office machines and equipment, 63-64
  operating abilities, 64
Telephone call, to and from prospective
  employer, 201
Temp work, 107-108
Testimonials, from previous employers, 45
Training, *see* Education and training
Training secretaries, sample job description
  for, 40
Transferable duties, for career changers 94-96

Typing
  sample job description for, 35-36
  skills, 18-19, 64, 170
  speed, 64, 170

Verbs, for describing job duties, 45-48

Want ads, matching skills to, 20-25
Women Secretaries' Association of
  Thailand, 205
Word lists, 46-48, 69-71
Word processing, 18, 35, 63
Work experience, *see* Job history
Work history, *see* Job history
Workforce, reentering after absence, *see*
  Reentering the workforce, individuals
Writing correspondence, sample job descrip-
  tion for, 39

About the Author

Rachel Lefkowitz, C.M.S., is a professional resume writer, office manager, and certified medical secretary with more than a decade of experience interviewing, hiring, and training office staff. She is a member of the Professional Association of Resume Writers and Professional Secretaries International, and provides secretaries and other office personnel with first-rate guidance on how to write standout resumes. In addition, as a health professional she has written and designed clinic brochures, health newsletters, and numerous other promotional materials. She makes her home in Thornhill, Ontario..